the VEGAN Bible

Publications International, Ltd.

Pictured on the front cover: Spring Vegetable Ragoût *(page 65).*

Pictured on the back cover *(clockwise from top left):* Rich Roasted Sesame Vegetables *(page 162),*
Seitan Fajitas *(page 126)* and Carrot Ginger Cupcakes *(page 170).*

Contributing Writer: Marilyn Pocius

Interior art on pages 9–19 by Dreamstime, Fotofolio, iStockphoto, PIL Collection, Shutterstock
and Thinkstock.

ISBN-13: 978-1-4508-7416-8
ISBN-10: 1-4508-7416-9

Library of Congress Control Number: 2013942057

Manufactured in China.

8 7 6 5 4 3 2 1

Microwave Cooking: Microwave ovens vary in wattage. Use the cooking times as guidelines and check
for doneness before adding more time.

Note: This book is for informational purposes and is not intended to provide medical advice. Neither
Publications International, Ltd., nor the authors, editors or publisher takes responsibility for any possible
consequences from any treatment, procedure, exercise, dietary modification, action, or applications of
medication or preparation by any person reading or following the information in this cookbook. The
publication of this book does not constitute the practice of medicine, and this cookbook does not replace
your physician, pharmacist or health-care specialist. **Before undertaking any course of treatment or
nutritional plan, the authors, editors and publisher advise the reader to check with a physician or
other health-care provider.**

Publications International, Ltd.

TABLE OF CONTENTS

Page 102

Page 112

Page 132

Page 185

The First Vegan

The word "vegan" was coined by Donald Watson, a British woodworker. Watson became a vegetarian at the age of 12 after seeing a pig slaughtered on his uncle's farm in Yorkshire England. He and his wife Dorothy founded the Vegan Society in 1944. Looking for a name for a vegetarian diet that also excluded other animal products, he put together letters from the beginning and end of the word "vegetarian" to spell "vegan," a word now found in most dictionaries.

The Pleasures of Vegan Cooking

Vegan, at least as defined for this book, means consuming no animal products—no meat, poultry, fish, dairy, eggs or honey. There are many different kinds of vegans and even more reasons for becoming one, from ethics to weight control. Of course there are also plenty of compelling health and environmental reasons for giving up animal products, but one of the unsung joys of cooking vegan dishes is the incredible flavor you'll discover—the plant kingdom offers so much variety in terms of color, taste and texture. When a meal isn't centered around meat, it's easier to appreciate the sweet tenderness of a roasted beet or the crunch of just-picked sugar snap peas. The recipes in this book were chosen to help make vegan cooking and eating not just healthy, but truly delicious. Becoming vegan should be about wonderful new dishes to discover, not about food you have to give up.

All Kinds of Vegans for All Kinds of Reasons

This book is not just for dedicated vegans but also for those who want to try out a new way to cook and eat. The recipes use no animal products—no meat, fish, dairy, eggs, honey or gelatin. Health is the most common reason for eating a plant-based diet. A diet filled with veggies, fruits, grains and nuts tends to be lower in fat and higher in fiber and antioxidants. Concern for animals is also a big part of the motivation. Many feel that it is morally indefensible to kill animals for food. For others, the very idea of meat becomes repulsive once they know about factory farms, mad-cow disease, E. coli contamination and the like.

A recent study estimates that 3.2 percent of the adults in the U.S. (about 7.3 million people) follow a vegetarian-based diet. Estimates put the number of vegans in that pool at about 1 million (and growing fast!). Millions more want the benefits of a vegan diet but aren't ready to commit to it 100 percent. Being vegan, at least some of the time, is being embraced by more and more people from rock stars to ex-presidents.

Becoming Vegan

It doesn't require a degree in nutrition, joining a club or giving up dinner with friends. Being on a vegan diet simply means that you don't eat anything that comes from an animal. Of course there are animal products other than food that are part of our lives—leather shoes, tallow in soap and lanolin in lip balm, for example. Those who espouse a totally vegan lifestyle often choose to avoid animal products in every part of their lives. This book only addresses the dietary part of the equation.

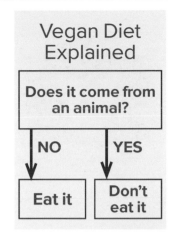

But What Will I Eat?

Gone are the days when a vegan had to visit a strange smelling, brightly lit health food store to buy provisions. Now any decent size market stocks soymilk, quinoa, veggie burgers and even seitan. Don't think about replacing meat; instead, consider all the wonderful vegetables, grains, fruits and nuts you will enjoy. A quick look through the recipes in this book will convince you that dishes like Mushroom Gratin (page 148) or Italian Escarole and White Bean Stew (page 66) are every bit as satisfying (and considerably better for you!) than another dinner of ground beef or chicken nuggets.

Planning Vegan Meals

For some time now, American meals have consisted of a main course—meat—accompanied by sides. The newly minted vegan may, at first, simply replace the center-of-the-plate meat with a veggie lasagna or tofu dog. A meal certainly doesn't have to be structured that way. It doesn't even have to be served on one big plate! In fact, most cuisines around the world are considerably less meat-centric. In Chinese and Japanese cooking, meat is more often a condiment or flavoring agent than the star of the show. The Middle East has its small plates called mezes and Spain specializes in tapas. Vegan meals work well as a series of individual dishes that complement each other without a single item stealing the show. Soup and salad can be a filling and delightful dinner. A colorful stir-fry could be the centerpiece for an elegant dinner party. The possibilities are endless.

Vegan FAQs

1 Isn't it hard to become vegan?
It can be if you try to change everything overnight. Instead approach it gradually and positively. Every day that you don't eat animal products is a step in the right direction for your health, animal welfare and the environment. You can start by going vegetarian first, or try going vegan for a few days a week.

2 Is a vegan diet expensive?
It certainly doesn't have to be. Meat is an expensive part of the typical American diet. Meat and dairy substitutes can be pricey, but seasonal produce, beans, rice and pasta are certainly affordable.

3 Must I take vitamin supplements?
Not necessarily. See page 8 for nutritional information. According to the American Dietetic Association, "…appropriately planned vegetarian diets, including total vegetarian or vegan diets, are healthful, nutritionally adequate, and may provide health benefits in the prevention and treatment of certain diseases."

4 What about organic foods?
Foods labeled organic have been raised according to standards protecting the environment, health and animal welfare. They are not necessarily vegan.

5 Do I have to give up chocolate?
Chocolate comes from a plant—the cocoa bean—so it starts out vegan. However, a lot of chocolate products have milk solids or milk fat added. The good news is that high-quality dark chocolate usually contains nothing more than cocoa, cocoa butter and sugar, so feel free to indulge.

6 What do I tell friends who invite me for dinner?
Explain that you don't eat animal products. Most cooks want to know about dietary preferences and are used to making allowances for vegetarians and those with food allergies. Just don't expect everything on the menu to be vegan.

7 What about eating out?
More and more restaurants offer vegetarian and even vegan menu options. Online sources can help you find those in your area. For fast food options, your best bets are Asian or Mexican eateries that will prepare a stir-fry or burrito to order.

8 But I love to bake. How can I do that without eggs or milk?
Don't despair or throw away your old cookbooks. Most recipes can easily be converted. See pages 10 – 11 for information on dairy and egg substitutes.

9 Will I lose weight?
Maybe, but the vegan diet isn't a weight loss program. If you give up meat but live on French fries, pasta and bread, you won't be doing your waistline or your health any good.

10 What about bread? Is yeast vegan?
Yeast is a one-celled fungus and just as vegan as a mushroom. In fact, yeast cells are in the air all around us, which is how naturally leavened breads are made. However, many packaged breads on supermarket shelves do contain milk products or eggs. Stick with European-style baguettes or ciabatta and read labels carefully.

The Healthy Vegan Diet

The key to any healthy diet is variety. A vegan diet consisting of pasta and potato chips would certainly not provide the vitamins, minerals and other nutrients human bodies need. A diet of fast food burgers, fried chicken and soda would be even worse! For vegans, variety means eating plenty of fruits, vegetables, leafy greens, whole grains, nuts, seeds and legumes.

More of the Good Stuff

Eliminating animal products from your diet gets rid of most sources of cholesterol and saturated fats. Better yet, without meat you'll probably eat more high-fiber grains, fruits and vegetables. Every food pyramid and healthy-eating expert agrees that eating a variety of colorful produce is good for you. Phytonutrients give food a rainbow of colors, and ongoing research seems to indicate they can be helpful in preventing disease and boosting immune systems. Carotinoids provide yellow and orange colors and are powerful antioxidants. Think carrots and squash. Tomatoes and watermelon are red because they contain lycopene, which may fight cancer. Resveratrol from purple grapes and wine is another antioxidant. There's no need to get a degree in nutrition—just enjoy a colorful variety of foods every day.

The Protein Problem That Isn't

If you've been a vegan for a while, you've probably been asked, "But what do you do about protein?" Our meat-centric society thinks of beef, pork, chicken and milk as the only good sources of protein. Plant foods actually provide plenty of protein—check the nutritional listings for tofu, lentils or quinoa if you need reassurance. Decades ago nutritionists believed that since meat contained all the essential amino acids (the ones our body can't produce on its own), vegetarians needed to eat a combination of foods at each meal that provided this same assortment. It was complicated and soon found to be totally unnecessary—your metabolism takes care of combining for you. In fact, most Americans eat too much protein, which can be unhealthy!

Tips to Keep Vegan Diets Interesting

1 Serve three or four small plates instead of one main course with sides.

2 Go ethnic. Explore Asian noodle dishes like Quick Szechuan Vegetable Lo Mein (page 98) or try Mexican bean dishes like Four-Pepper Black Bean Fajitas (page 134).

3 Give potatoes and pasta a rest. Try adding couscous, quinoa or bulgur wheat instead.

4 Experiment with meat replacements. In addition to tofu, try tempeh, seitan or texturized soy protein (pages 12–13).

5 Cook with the seasons. Take advantage of farmers' markets and enjoy more fresh produce.

6 Go nuts! Spread nut butters on your toast. Add toasted almonds or walnuts to your cereal, salad, casserole or stir-fry.

Know Your Nutrients

Here's a list of good sources of nutrients sometimes lacking in a vegan diet.

Protein
legumes
lentils
soy products
whole grains

Calcium
almonds
broccoli
fortified orange juice
kale
tahini
tofu

Vitamin B$_{12}$
enriched dairy-free milks
enriched nutritional yeast
fortified cereals

Omega-3 Fatty Acids
flaxseed
olive oil
tofu
walnuts

Iron*
brussels sprouts
blackstrap molasses
edamame
kidney beans
lentils
turmeric

To enhance iron absorption, combine foods with those rich in Vitamin C.

Important Nutrients for Vegans

Calcium and Vitamin D
Do we need drink to milk to get enough calcium as the dairy industry tries to convince us? Fortunately there are many plant sources for calcium; many of them provide magnesium and potassium as well, which are also vital for bone health. Collard greens, tahini, broccoli and fortified dairy-free milk are just a few plant sources of calcium. Vitamin D is also necessary for strong bones. Exposure to sunlight is one way to get it. The only plant source is mushrooms, but Vitamin D is also often added to fortified dairy-free milks, cereals and orange juice.

Vitamin B$_{12}$
Vitamin B$_{12}$ is found only in animal foods. Fortunately there are many vegan foods that are fortified with this important vitamin responsible for cell division and blood formation. Check labels, but dairy-free milks, cereals, meat substitutes and nutritional yeast are often fortified. You can also take a supplement. The good news is that we require only a small amount of B$_{12}$ and can store and recycle it. However, absorption rates of B$_{12}$ from food or supplements can vary from 50 percent to 0.5 percent. Consult a doctor or nutritionist if you are concerned.

Omega-3 Fatty Acids
There are three different types of omega-3 fatty acids. ALA is found in plant sources like flaxseed, tofu and walnuts. The other two types are EPA and DHA, which come from oily fish. DHA is the type that is most researched and seems to have the most health benefits. Our bodies can convert ALA into the beneficial DHA but it requires more metabolic work, so you need to consume more ALA if you are vegan to achieve the same level of DHA as a fish eater. There are vegan DHA supplements available made from algae.

Iron
There are many plant sources of iron, including dried fruits, nuts, green leafy vegetables, beans, whole grains and blackstrap molasses. Using cast iron pots and pans can also contribute iron to the food cooked in them. Now aren't you glad you're a vegan and don't have to take your cod liver oil?

The Vegan Pantry

All cooking depends on the quality of ingredients—even more so if it's vegan. The sometimes subtle flavors of fresh produce need to be coaxed and complemented, not overwhelmed. Use cheap oil or a dusty jar of dried basil and it will be easy to tell. The flavor of meat can mask a multitude of sins!

For the recipes in this book, here are some pantry items you should keep on hand:

Agave nectar

Beans: a variety of canned and/or dried

Bulgur wheat

Chickpeas

Dairy-free milk and margarine

Egg replacer, powdered

Ground flaxseed

Lentils

Mushrooms: fresh and dried

Noodles and pasta

Nutritional yeast

Nuts: almonds, cashews, walnuts

Oils: extra virgin olive oil, vegetable oil

Rice: long grain, brown, basmati, jasmine

Soy foods: edamame, miso paste, soy sauce, tempeh, texturized soy protein, tofu

Tomatoes: canned whole and diced

Advanced Label Reading

Skip over the advertising claims on package labels like "natural", "cruelty-free" and "earth friendly." These are generally meaningless. The real information is in the ingredient list in very small type. It's easy to spot meat, eggs and dairy, but multisyllabic names hidden in a lengthy list can make recognizing animal ingredients a lot trickier. Generally the longer the list, the more processed the food item, and the more likely it is to contain animal products.

Often dairy products in some form are added to commercial baked goods to improve shelf life and texture. They can be listed as casein, whey or lactose. You can always query the manufacturer or check one an online list of suspect ingredients.

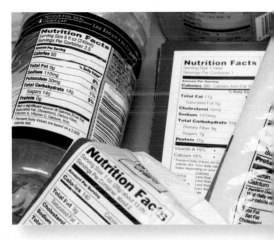

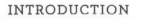

Cooking Minus the Moo

Giving up milk products is often the biggest challenge for vegans. It's easy to forget that dairy is so integral to many favorites, from the cheese on pizza to the butter in cookies. Not to mention that casein and whey, both dairy products, show up in margarine, soy cheeses and other vegetarian products. Fortunately, U.S. food manufacturers are now required to list the simple word "milk" as part of the ingredient list or in boldface type at the end of the list, even if the actual dairy ingredient goes by an obscure chemical name. The really good news is that there are more and better dairy replacement products available all the time.

Nondairy is NOT always Dairy-Free

Many products labeled nondairy contain whey, casein or other milk-derived ingredients. According to the FDA, nondairy products can contain 0.5 percent or less of milk products by weight. Nondairy creamers and nondairy whipped toppings usually contain dairy in some form.

Dairy-Free Milk

Once soymilk was your only choice. Now you can try rice milk, almond milk, coconut milk, oat milk, even hemp milk. These tasty dairy replacements can do pretty much everything milk can do. While dairy-free milks can be substituted for each other, the different flavors and textures may influence how you use them. Rice milk is slightly sweet, so it works well in dessert recipes but is not as appropriate in savory dishes. Soymilk is a good substitute in baking since it is similar to cow's milk in protein content and texture. Almond milk is rich and nutty but has a flavor profile that can clash with savory dishes.

When choosing a dairy-free milk, check the nutritional label. Most are fortified with calcium and vitamin B_{12} to bring them nutritionally closer to cow's milk. You may also want to check protein and sugar content, which vary.

Dairy-Free Margarine

Warning: Most regular margarines contain small amounts of milk products, even those labeled nondairy. Look for the word "vegan", "dairy-free" or the Kosher designation "pareve" or "parv," which means no dairy products at all. Dairy-free margarine comes in two forms: in sticks like butter and in tubs. The stick form can be used one-to-one to replace butter in baking recipes. Tub margarine often contains more water or air, so it will not measure the same as stick margarine or butter.

Dairy-Free Sour Cream and Yogurt

A little tangy sour cream or yogurt goes a long way to make dips and smoothies more satisfying, and a dollop on spicy stews can help cool the fire. A few years ago, vegan options were quite limited, but as the vegan diet has become more mainstream, more products have become available. Many dairy-free yogurts are also cultured or fortified to provide helpful probiotics.

But What About Cheese?!

Let's admit that cheese is one of the toughest things to replace. Sure, there are dairy-free cheeses, but many of them don't taste like the real thing and quite a few soy cheeses have casein added to help them melt better, so check the labels. There are more and better choices all the time, so experiment with different brands to find one you like best.

For bland cheeses like ricotta or cottage cheese, crumbled tofu is often a good stand-in. You'll also find recipes online for making your own spreadable vegan cheese from cashews or macadamia nuts, and nutritional yeast adds a savory tang to many recipes and can be sprinkled on popcorn or pasta like Parmesan cheese.

Baking without Butter or Eggs

For most recipes the easiest replacement for butter is vegan margarine. Unrefined coconut oil, which is solid at room temperature like butter, is another option where the slight coconut flavor works. For pie crusts, choose a vegan or non-hydrogenated vegetable shortening.

The easiest and most consistent replacement for eggs in baked goods is powdered egg replacer—simply mix it with water according to package directions. In most baked goods requiring no more than three eggs, silken tofu is also an acceptable replacement. (Use ¼ cup to replace each egg.) Ground flaxseed is another possible substitute: Thoroughly blend 1 tablespoon ground flaxseed with 3 tablespoons water for each egg; heat in a small saucepan over low heat until thickened. Cool completely. One mashed banana or ¼ cup of applesauce can often fill in for one egg in quick breads or muffins that are sweet or fruity.

When Is an Egg Substitute Not a Substitute?

The little cartons often labeled "egg substitute" in the dairy case are usually egg whites, created to allow people to enjoy eggs without the cholesterol found in the yolks. They are not vegan.

What is Nutritional Yeast?

It's not for making bread rise! Nutritional yeast is a favorite with vegetarians, especially vegans, since it has a taste similar to Parmesan cheese and can be a source of vitamin B_{12}. It is a deactivated yeast that comes in powder or flake form and can be sprinkled directly on food or used in recipes. Read labels carefully though, since only a few brands are fortified with B_{12}; look for the tongue twister cyanocobalamin (the chemical name for B_{12}).

Tofu and Friends

Sometimes tofu, seitan and tempeh are referred to as meat substitutes. It's true that these ingredients can be made into products that resemble meat with a satisfying chew and somewhat meaty flavor. However, many vegans enjoy them because they are delicious and nutritious in and of themselves. While they are relatively recent additions to American kitchens, they have been a huge part of Asian cuisines for centuries.

TOFU

You probably know that tofu is made from soybeans, but you may be unaware that the process that produces it is very similar to making cheese. A salt- or acid-based coagulant is added to soymilk to form curds and whey. (Remember Little Miss Muffet?) Once the curds are drained and pressed you have a block of tofu.

Using Tofu

Tofu comes in many forms, as a visit to any Asian market will illustrate, but there are two main types. Regular or brick tofu (sometimes called Chinese tofu) is sold in the refrigerated section of the supermarket in the produce section or near the dairy case and comes sealed in a plastic tub filled with water. There is usually a choice of soft, medium, firm or extra firm. Once opened, regular tofu will keep in the refrigerator up to four days. The water should be drained and replaced daily. Silken tofu, sometimes called Japanese tofu, usually comes in an aseptic box, which does not require refrigeration. While it also comes in soft, medium or firm, the texture of silken tofu is almost custard-like compared to regular. It is an excellent thickener and works well in soups. Silken tofu is too delicate to use in most stir-fries where it will crumble and dissolve.

TEMPEH

Tempeh (pronounced "TEM-pay") is a very nutritious fermented soy food that originated in Indonesia hundreds of years ago. Although it won't win prizes for good looks—it looks like a messy cake of beans and nuts squashed together—tempeh has a nutty, yeasty flavor and chewy texture that is easy to love. You'll find cakes of tempeh, vacuum-packed and refrigerated, in natural food stores and some supermarkets. Soybean tempeh is the classic version, but tempeh can also be made of rice and other grains, or be a mixture of soy and grain.

Using Tempeh
It's best to cook tempeh before eating it, although this is for taste reasons rather than food safety ones. Cooking improves both flavor and texture.

Like tofu, tempeh has an ability to readily absorb flavors and cooking enhances this. Its firm texture makes it a great choice to replace ground beef, cook on the grill or use in a sandwich.

SEITAN
Seitan (pronounced "SAY-tan") is sometimes called wheat-meat, gluten-meat or mock duck. It is made by washing away the starch component from wheat until only the wheat protein—gluten—is left. If you've ever eaten mock duck or mock chicken in a Chinese restaurant, you've tried seitan. It is also the base for some commercial vegetarian deli "meats."

Using Seitan
You'll find seitan in the refrigerated section of natural food stores and large supermakets near the produce section or the dairy case in a tub or a vacuum pack. It may also be found in the freezer section. Varieties are plain, flavored, Asian-style with soy and ginger, or seasoned to taste like chicken or other meat. Seitan is incredibly versatile. It can be stir-fried, baked, broiled or grilled.

TEXTURED SOY PROTEIN (TVP)
Textured soy protein is defatted soy flour and a by-product of extracting the oil from soybeans. It comes in granules, flakes, chunks and nuggets. It has a protein content and texture similar to ground beef when reconstituted.

Using Textured Soy Protein
To use textured soy protein it must be soaked briefly in a hot liquid. (See the recipe for Vegan Sloppy Joes on page 82.) Use granulated TVP as a substitute for ground meat in tacos, chili or pasta sauce, or form it into veggie burgers or meatballs. Larger chunks can stand in for meat in casseroles, stews or chilies.

Going with the Grain

Grains are the center of the plate in many cultures. Asian cuisine is built around rice. In Thailand the traditional greeting translates as, "Have you eaten rice yet?" Italy has pasta made from durum wheat. In both North and South America, corn was central to ancient cuisine and culture. Bread and cereal are certainly mainstays of our lives, but there are more kinds of grains available now than ever before, and there are delicious options that go way beyond a loaf of white bread.

Storing Grains

Whole grains are considerably more nutritious than processed ones, but since they contain the oil-rich germ as well as the bran, they become rancid much more quickly. It's best to store what you won't use up in several months in the refrigerator or freezer. Buy small quantities of an assortment of grains and keep them in covered containers labeled with the date they were purchased. If you are buying from bulk bins, take a good sniff first. Grain should smell sweet and earthy not stale or rancid. Grains that are past their prime not only don't taste good, they take longer to cook.

Barley

Slightly sweet, nutty and chewy, barley is easy to love and makes a good substitute for rice. Pearl (pearled) barley, which is the most available kind, has been polished to remove its tough outer hull. Hulled or Scotch barley has more of the bran intact so it is more nutritious but also takes longer to cook.

Bulgur Wheat

To make bulgur wheat, whole kernels are steamed, dried and ground to varying degrees. The fine grind, which is the most common type, is ready in a matter of minutes. Bulgur is traditionally served cold in tabbouleh salad, but its fluffy texture also makes it a natural for soaking up juices or broths.

Cornmeal/Polenta

Polenta is the Italian name for a creamy porridge made from cornmeal that is eaten hot or cooled, sliced and fried. The American version of this dish is called cornmeal mush. It's easy to see why it never caught on under that name! Polenta is most nutritious and flavorful if prepared from whole grain, stone-ground cornmeal.

Couscous

We call couscous a grain, but it's actually a form of tiny pasta made from wheat flour. Whole wheat couscous is just as convenient as regular since it cooks in the same amount of time.

Farro

This ancient grain, which is part of the wheat family, is making a comeback among chefs and foodies. With its chewy texture and nutty flavor it's easy to see why. Swap farro for rice or barley in soups or stews. You can even use it in place of arborio rice in risotto recipes, though it will have a different texture.

Millet

Mild-mannered millet has small beadlike grains that cook quickly. Once considered "for the birds," millet is being recognized for its pleasant cornlike flavor and good nutritional profile—millet is rich in B vitamins.

Quinoa

If you're only going to add one new grain to your meals, make it quinoa. The Incas considered it sacred and called it the mother of all grains. Quinoa has also been called a supergrain since it is rich in protein, contains all essential amino acids, and is a good source of fiber, magnesium and iron. It is also easy to digest, has a sweet subtle taste and cooks in about 15 minutes!

Rice

Brown rice is whole grain rice with the nutrients in the bran or germ intact. There are many varieties of rice and they are often categorized by the length of their grains. Long-grain rice is at least three times longer than it is wide. These rices include the aromatic jasmine and basmati rices. Short-grain rice has plumper, rounder grains that tend to stick together more when cooked. Sushi rice and arborio rice are two examples. Rice that is especially sticky is often used in Asian desserts and is sometimes labeled sweet or glutinous rice, despite the fact that it contains no gluten!

Wheat Berries

These kernels of wheat are sold under the name whole wheat or wheat berries. They have a hearty, nutty flavor and satisfying chewiness. Wheat berries can take up to an hour to cook, but the time can be shortened by presoaking.

Grains as Convenience Foods

It's true that whole grains take time to cook, but there's an easy way to enjoy them even on a busy weeknight: Stockpile! Instead of preparing just 1 cup of rice, barley or wheat berries, double or triple the amount you need and store the rest for another meal. Cooked grains will keep for several days in the refrigerator and for months in the freezer.

The Kernel of the Matter

All grains have three parts: a tough outer layer that protects the grain called the bran; the starchy endosperm that makes up the biggest portion of the kernel; and the germ or the embryo of the grain at its base. The bran and the germ contain the most fiber and nutrients; they are often removed when grain is processed. Whole grains still contain all three parts.

The Beauty of Beans

Vegans know that beans count! They provide protein, fiber, amino acids and B vitamins to plant-based diets. Beans are also inexpensive and come in a kaleidoscope of colors and shapes. They can be enjoyed in every kind of dish from dips and salads to soups and stews to hearty main courses. In Asia, sweetened red beans are dessert—they are used to fill pastries and even make ice cream!

Adzuki Beans

These small, dark red beans are slightly sweet and creamy when cooked. They are the basis for sweet red bean paste used in Asian desserts.

Black Beans (turtle beans, frijoles negros)

Black beans are a staple of Latin American dishes. Their strong, earthy flavor and firm texture help them stand out in soups, salads and all sorts of side dishes.

Cannellini Beans (white kidney beans)

Mild-tasting meaty cannellinis are often used in minestrone soup and other Italian dishes.

Chickpeas (garbanzo beans)

The versatile chickpea has an almost buttery flavor and is a nutritional powerhouse with more than 80 nutrients, plus plenty of fiber and protein. Many classic vegetarian dishes, including hummus and falafel, start with chickpeas.

Kidney Beans

Kidney beans are full flavored and retain their kidney shape even with long cooking times. Take note that they also provide iron, an essential nutrient that is hard to get from vegetable sources. They come in dark red, light red, pink or white (see cannellini beans).

Lentils

Lentils cook quickly and are often served puréed. The most common varieties are brown and red, but for a larger selection explore the many different kinds used in Indian or Middle Eastern cuisines.

Lima Beans (butter beans)

Pale green limas are starchy and satisfying. If you've only had canned, give them another chance. Their rich buttery flavor holds up better when they're fresh or frozen.

Pinto Beans

Speckled beige beans with darker streaks, pintos are used for refried beans, chili and many Mexican recipes. Unfortunately their pretty markings—"pinto" means painted in Spanish—turn dull pinkish beige after cooking.

White Beans (Great Northern, navy beans)

These mild, meaty beans are favorites in casseroles, stews and soups. They are fiber superstars. A single cup of navy beans provides more than 75 percent of the recommended daily value!

Dried Bean Basics

Cooking dried beans is easy and economical and produces firmer, tastier beans. It does take more time than opening a can, but most of it is unsupervised.

1 **Buy the right beans.** Old beans or those that have been stored in heat or humidity will never cook correctly. (Throw away that old package that's been in your cupboard for five years right now!) Purchase beans from a place that has a high turnover. Choose beans that are brightly colored with smooth skins.

2 **Soak.** Sort through the beans and discard any broken ones or foreign matter while rinsing them thoroughly. Place in a nonreactive bowl or pan and cover with fresh cold water by about 3 inches. Toss any beans that float. Soak at least four hours or overnight until the bean skins get wrinkled. (There is no need to soak lentils.)

3 **Cook.** Drain the beans and rinse them. Place them in a saucepan and cover with fresh cold water by at least 1 inch. Bring the beans to a boil and skim any foam that rises to the top. Cover and simmer the beans over low heat for 45 minutes to 2 hours or until tender but not mushy. Timing will depend on the variety of bean and also how long it was stored. Add hot water if needed to keep the beans covered. Add salt and seasonings when the beans are almost tender.

What's the difference between a bean and a legume?

Legumes are a class of vegetable that includes beans, peas and lentils, all of which grow in pods. What about green beans? When the entire pod is eaten, the plant is considered a green vegetable.

Bean Counting

One pound of dried beans will yield four to five cups of cooked beans, or approximately 8 servings. A 15-ounce can contains 1 ½ to 2 cups of cooked beans, depending on the variety.

Quick Vegan Ice Cream

Combine 2 cans unsweetened coconut milk and ½ cup sugar in medium saucepan. Cook over medium-low heat, whisking constantly, until smooth. Refrigerate until cold. Process in an ice cream maker according to manufacturer's directions. Add chocolate chips or fruit during the last few minutes of processing, if you like.

Kale Chips

Preheat oven to 375°F. Tear leaves into 1-inch pieces. Toss with a little olive oil and seasoned salt, spread in a single layer on a baking sheet and bake about 10 minutes or until crisp.

Very Vegan, Very Delicious

Most people who say they can't imagine what vegans eat lack imagination themselves! The plant kingdom offers choices of color, texture and taste that go way beyond the dull beige world of meat. Here are some ideas for adding flavor and fun to your vegan diet.

Agar Agar

This amazing ingredient can do anything gelatin can do better and without animal products. It's made from seaweed and has been used in Asian cuisines for centuries. Agar agar has little taste of its own, so it works in sweet or savory dishes. It will set at room temperature and stay set when warm. In addition, it retains some of the nutrients of seaweed.

Agave Nectar

This natural sweetener is made from a cactus-like plant. Agave nectar has a delicate flavor and syrupy consistency, which make it an excellent substitute for honey or white sugar.

Coconut Milk

Coconut milk makes a rich, creamy vegan substitute for milk products in cooking. Look for unsweetened coconut milk in cans in the Asian section of the supermarket. (Coconut water is a much thinner liquid and is sold for drinking, not cooking.)

Flaxseed

Versatile flaxseed is rich in alpha linolenic acid, the plant version of omega-3 fatty acids. Add ground flaxseed to hot or cold cereal, a smoothie or soy yogurt. Add it to baked goods or use it as an egg replacer (see page 11).

Kale

Finally kale has become trendy and is being appreciated for more than just its excellent nutritional profile. Add kale to any pasta, potato, grain or bean dish for color and flavor. Enjoy the frilly green leaves in a salad, simmered or sautéed.

Miso

This fermented soy-based seasoning paste has a buttery texture and a tangy, salty taste. In addition to soup (see page 64 for a recipe), miso is also used for dressings, marinades and sauces.

Nutritional Yeast

It won't make bread rise or expand in your tummy because it's an inactive version of yeast, but this magical ingredient is a favorite with many vegans. Nutritional yeast has a nutty, cheesy flavor and is used in countless recipes for cheese sauces, pastas, gravies, tofu and meatless patties.

Sesame Seeds

They may be tiny, but sesame seeds open up a word of flavors and textures wherever they go. Add toasted sesame seeds to salads, cereals and vegetables. Tahini, a paste made from sesame seeds, is a necessary ingredient in hummus and can also be used as a spread for sandwiches.

Shiitake Mushrooms

The complex flavor of shiitake mushrooms blends a touch of smoke with a hint of pine and autumn leaves. This rich savoriness can elevate vegetable or grain dishes to gourmet status.

Walnuts

Along with a delectable flavor and delicious crunch, walnuts provide a good source of hard-to-get omega-3 fatty acids. Add them to pancake batters, cookies, breads and salads. Because they are high in protein and fiber, walnuts also make a satisfying snack.

Vegan "Parmesan"

Combine equal parts almonds, nutritional yeast and bread crumbs in a food processor. Pulse to combine and add salt to taste. Use as a topping for pizza, salad or vegetables.

Tahini Sauce

Whisk ½ cup tahini, ¼ cup lemon juice, ¼ cup olive oil, plus minced garlic, cumin, salt and pepper. Add water to thicken to desired consistency. Serve with falafel or steamed veggies.

BREAKFAST & BRUNCH

apple-cinnamon breakfast risotto

¼ cup (½ stick) dairy-free magarine

4 medium Granny Smith apples, peeled and diced (about 1½ pounds)

1½ teaspoons ground cinnamon

¼ teaspoon salt

¼ teaspoon ground allspice

1½ cups uncooked arborio rice

½ cup packed dark brown sugar

4 cups unfiltered apple juice,* at room temperature

1 teaspoon vanilla

Dairy-free milk (optional)

Sliced almonds and dried cranberries (optional)

If unfiltered apple juice is unavailable, use any apple juice.

Slow Cooker Directions

1 Melt margarine in large skillet over medium-high heat. Add apples, cinnamon, salt and allspice; cook and stir 3 to 5 minutes or until apples begin to soften.

2 Combine apple mixture and rice in slow cooker; stir to coat. Sprinkle with brown sugar. Add apple juice and vanilla. Cover; cook on HIGH 1½ to 2 hours or until all liquid is absorbed.

3 Spoon risotto into six serving bowls. Serve with dairy-free milk; top with almonds and cranberries, if desired.

Makes 6 servings

NOTE: Arborio rice, an Italian-grown short-grain rice, has a delicious nutty taste. It is traditionally used for risotto dishes because its high starch content produces a creamy texture.

vegan pancakes

2 cups soymilk or other dairy-free milk

2 tablespoons lemon juice

2 tablespoons vegetable oil

1 tablespoon agave nectar

1 cup all-purpose flour

1 cup spelt flour

1 teaspoon baking soda

1 teaspoon baking powder

½ teaspoon salt

1 to 2 tablespoons dairy-free magarine, melted

Fresh fruit and/or maple syrup

1 Combine soymilk and lemon juice in large measuring cup or medium bowl. Let stand 5 minutes. Stir in oil and agave.

2 Whisk all-purpose flour, spelt flour, baking soda, baking powder and salt in large bowl. Whisk in soymilk mixture until fairly smooth. (Some lumps will remain.)

3 Heat large nonstick skillet or griddle over medium-high heat. Brush lightly with margarine. Pour batter into skillet in 4-inch circles. Cook 3 to 5 minutes or until edges of pancakes become dull and bubbles form on tops. Flip pancakes; cook 1 to 2 minutes or until browned. Keep warm. Serve with fruit or maple syrup.

Makes about 14 pancakes

tofu peanut butter smoothie

1 banana, cut into chunks

½ cup soft tofu

¼ cup creamy peanut butter

1 to 2 ice cubes

1 teaspoon vanilla

Combine banana, tofu, peanut butter, ice and vanilla in blender; blend until smooth. Pour into glass; serve immediately.

Makes 1 (8-ounce) serving

vegan pancakes

scrambled tofu and potatoes

Potatoes

- ¼ cup olive oil
- 4 to 5 red potatoes, cubed
- ½ white onion, sliced
- 1 tablespoon chopped fresh rosemary
- 1 teaspoon coarse salt

Scrambled Tofu

- ¼ cup nutritional yeast
- ½ teaspoon ground turmeric
- 2 tablespoons water
- 2 tablespoons soy sauce
- 1 package (14 ounces) firm tofu
- 2 teaspoons olive oil
- ½ cup chopped green bell pepper
- ½ cup chopped red onion
- 2 green onions, chopped

1 For potatoes, preheat oven to 450°F. Add ¼ cup olive oil to 12-inch cast-iron skillet; place skillet in oven 10 minutes to heat.

2 Bring large saucepan of water to a boil. Add potatoes; cook 5 to 7 minutes or until potatoes are tender. Drain potatoes and return to saucepan; stir in white onion, rosemary and salt. Spread mixture in preheated skillet. Bake 25 to 30 minutes or until potatoes are browned, stirring every 10 minutes.

3 For tofu, combine nutritional yeast and turmeric in small bowl. Stir in water and soy sauce until smooth.

4 Cut tofu into 8 cubes. Gently squeeze out water; loosely crumble tofu into medium bowl. Heat 2 teaspoons olive oil in large skillet over medium-high heat. Add bell pepper and red onion; cook and stir 2 minutes or until soft but not browned. Add tofu; drizzle with 3 tablespoons nutritional yeast sauce. Cook and stir about 5 minutes or until liquid is evaporated and tofu is uniformly colored and heated through. Stir in additional sauce, if desired, for stronger flavor.

5 Divide potatoes among four serving plates. Top with tofu; sprinkle with green onions.

Makes 4 servings

boston black coffee bread

½ cup rye flour

½ cup cornmeal

½ cup whole wheat flour

1 teaspoon baking soda

½ teaspoon salt

¾ cup strong brewed coffee, room temperature or cold

⅓ cup molasses

¼ cup canola oil

¾ cup raisins

1 Preheat oven to 325°F. Grease and flour 9×5-inch loaf pan.

2 Combine rye flour, cornmeal, whole wheat flour, baking soda and salt in large bowl. Stir in coffee, molasses and oil until blended. Fold in raisins. Pour batter into prepared pan.

3 Bake 50 minutes or until toothpick inserted into center comes out clean. Cool in pan on wire rack.

Makes 10 servings

TIP: To cool hot coffee, pour it over 2 ice cubes in a measuring cup to measure ¾ cup total. Let stand 10 minutes.

pear-avocado smoothie

1 pear, peeled and cubed

1 cup apple juice

1 cup ice cubes

½ avocado, peeled and pitted

½ cup fresh mint leaves

2 tablespoon lime juice

Combine pear, apple juice, ice, avocado, mint and lime juice in blender or food processor; blend until smooth. Pour into two glasses; serve immediately.

Makes 2 (8-ounce) servings

blueberry poppy seed coffeecake

¾ cup plain soymilk or other dairy-free milk

1 tablespoon lemon juice or vinegar

1½ cups all-purpose flour

½ cup sugar

1 teaspoon baking powder

½ teaspoon baking soda

¼ teaspoon salt

¼ cup (½ stick) cold dairy-free margarine, cut into small pieces

1 tablespoon poppy seeds

Prepared egg replacer equal to 1 egg

1 teaspoon grated lemon peel

1 teaspoon vanilla

1 cup fresh blueberries

1 Preheat oven to 350°F. Spray 9-inch round cake pan with nonstick cooking spray. Combine soymilk and lemon juice in measuring cup. Let stand 5 minutes.

2 Combine flour, sugar, baking powder, baking soda and salt in large bowl. Cut in margarine with pastry blender or two knives until mixture resembles coarse crumbs. Stir in poppy seeds.

3 Whisk soymilk mixture, egg replacer, lemon peel and vanilla in small bowl until blended. Stir into flour mixture just until combined. Spread half of batter in prepared pan; top with blueberries. Drop remaining batter in dollops over blueberries, leaving some berries uncovered.

4 Bake 33 to 36 minutes or until top is golden brown. Cool 15 minutes in pan on wire rack. Serve warm.

Makes 8 servings

banana bran bread

1 cup bran cereal

½ cup boiling water

1⅓ cups all-purpose flour

½ cup sugar

1 teaspoon baking powder

½ teaspoon baking soda

½ teaspoon salt

¼ teaspoon ground cinnamon

2 tablespoons vegetable oil

Prepared egg replacer
equal to 2 eggs

1 cup mashed ripe bananas
(2 medium to large
bananas)

¼ cup crumbled unsweetened
banana chips

1 Preheat oven to 350°F. Spray 8×4-inch loaf pan with nonstick cooking spray.

2 Place cereal in medium bowl; stir in boiling water. Let stand 10 minutes.

3 Combine flour, sugar, baking powder, baking soda, salt and cinnamon in large bowl. Whisk oil and egg replacer in small bowl; add to flour mixture. Stir in bran mixture and mashed bananas. Spoon batter into prepared pan; sprinkle with banana chips.

4 Bake 45 to 50 minutes or until toothpick inserted into center comes out clean. Cool in pan 5 minutes; remove to wire rack to cool completely.

Makes 8 servings

crispy skillet potatoes

2 tablespoons olive oil

4 red potatoes, cut
into thin wedges

½ cup chopped onion

2 tablespoons lemon pepper

½ teaspoon coarse salt

1 Heat oil in large skillet over medium heat. Stir in potatoes, onion, lemon pepper and salt.

2 Cover and cook 25 to 30 minutes or until potatoes are tender and browned, turning occasionally.

Makes 4 servings

banana bran bread

breakfast quinoa

½ cup uncooked quinoa

1 cup water

1 tablespoon packed brown sugar

2 teaspoons maple syrup

½ teaspoon ground cinnamon

¼ cup golden raisins (optional)

Dairy-free milk

Raspberries and banana slices

1 Place quinoa in fine-mesh strainer; rinse well under cold running water. Transfer to small saucepan.

2 Stir in water, brown sugar, maple syrup and cinnamon; bring to a boil over high heat. Reduce heat to low; cover and simmer 10 to 15 minutes or until quinoa is tender and water is absorbed. Add raisins, if desired, during last 5 minutes of cooking. Serve with dairy-free milk; top with raspberries and bananas.

Makes 2 servings

superfoods smoothie

1 cup coarsely chopped kale

1 cup baby spinach

1 cup ice cubes

1 banana

½ cup apple juice

Combine kale, spinach, ice, banana and apple juice in blender or food processor; blend until smooth. Pour into two glasses; serve immediately.

Makes 2 (6-ounce) servings

APPETIZERS & SNACKS

edamame hummus

1 package (16 ounces) frozen shelled edamame, thawed

2 green onions, coarsely chopped (about ½ cup)

½ cup loosely packed fresh cilantro leaves

3 to 4 tablespoons water

2 tablespoons canola oil

1½ tablespoons fresh lime juice

1 tablespoon agave nectar

2 cloves garlic

1 teaspoon salt

¼ teaspoon black pepper

Rice crackers or cut-up vegetables

1 Combine edamame, green onions, cilantro, 3 tablespoons water, oil, lime juice, agave, garlic, salt and pepper in food processor; process until smooth. Add additional water to thin dip, if necessary.

2 Serve with rice crackers or vegetables for dipping. Store in refrigerator up to 4 days.

Makes 2 cups

roasted sweet potato and hoisin lettuce wraps

1 to 2 large sweet potatoes (about 12 ounces), cut into ½-inch cubes

1 onion, cut into 8 wedges

1 tablespoon vegetable oil

Hoisin Dressing (recipe follows)

12 large Bibb lettuce leaves, rinsed and patted dry

2 cups shredded cabbage or packaged coleslaw

½ cup matchstick carrots*

½ cup toasted peanuts

Matchstick carrots are sometimes called shredded carrots and may be sold with other prepared vegetables in the supermarket produce section.

1 Preheat oven to 425°F. Line baking sheet with foil.

2 Place potatoes and onion on baking sheet; drizzle with oil and toss to coat. Roast 20 minutes or until edges of onion begin to brown and sweet potatoes are tender, stirring once halfway through cooking time.

3 Meanwhile, prepare Hoisin Dressing; set aside.

4 To serve, top each lettuce leaf with cabbage, sweet potato mixture and carrots. Drizzle with 1 tablespoon dressing; sprinkle with peanuts. Fold bottom over filling, then fold two sides up to form bundles.

Makes 4 servings

hoisin dressing

¼ cup water

¼ cup creamy peanut butter

3 tablespoons hoisin sauce

2 tablespoons lime juice

3 cloves garlic, minced

1 tablespoon vegetable oil

1 tablespoon ketchup

2 teaspoons grated fresh ginger

⅛ teaspoon red pepper flakes

Whisk water, peanut butter, hoisin sauce, lime juice, garlic, oil, ketchup, ginger and red pepper flakes in medium bowl until well blended.

Makes about ¾ cup

socca (niçoise chickpea pancake)

1 cup chickpea flour

¾ teaspoon salt

½ teaspoon black pepper

1 cup water

5 tablespoons olive oil, divided

1½ teaspoons minced fresh basil *or* ½ teaspoon dried basil

1 teaspoon minced fresh rosemary *or* ¼ teaspoon dried rosemary

¼ teaspoon dried thyme

1 Sift chickpea flour into medium bowl. Stir in salt and pepper. Gradually whisk in water until smooth. Stir in 2 tablespoons oil. Let stand at least 30 minutes.

2 Preheat oven to 450°F. Place 9- or 10-inch cast iron skillet in oven to heat.

3 Add basil, rosemary and thyme to batter; whisk until smooth. Carefully remove skillet from oven. Add 2 tablespoons oil to skillet, swirling to coat pan evenly. Immediately pour in batter.

4 Bake 12 to 15 minutes or until edge of pancake begins to pull away from side of pan and center is firm. Remove from oven. Preheat broiler.

5 Brush pancake with remaining 1 tablespoon oil. Broil 2 to 4 minutes or until dark brown in spots. Cut into wedges. Serve warm.

Makes 6 servings

NOTE: Socca is commonly served in paper cones as a savory street food in the south of France, especially around Nice.

TIP: To make a thinner, softer crêpe, just increase the amount of water in the recipe by about ¼ cup and cook in batches in a skillet.

guacamole cones

6 (6-inch) flour tortillas

1 tablespoon vegetable oil

1 teaspoon chili powder

2 ripe avocados

1½ tablespoons fresh lime juice

1 tablespoon finely chopped green onion

¼ teaspoon salt

¼ teaspoon black pepper

Dash hot pepper sauce (optional)

2 to 3 plum tomatoes, chopped

1 Preheat oven to 350°F. Line baking sheet with parchment paper.

2 Cut tortillas in half. Roll each tortilla half into cone shape; secure with toothpick. Brush outside of each cone with oil; sprinkle lightly with chili powder. Place on prepared baking sheet.

3 Bake 9 minutes or until cones are lightly browned. Turn cones upside down; bake about 5 minutes or until golden brown on all sides. Cool cones 1 minute; remove toothpicks and cool completely.

4 Cut avocados in half; remove and discard pits. Scoop avocado pulp from skins and place in medium bowl; mash with fork. Stir in lime juice, green onion, salt, pepper and hot pepper sauce, if desired, until blended.

5 Place 1 tablespoon chopped tomato in each tortilla cone; top with small scoop of guacamole and additional chopped tomatoes. Serve immediately.

Makes 12 cones

vegetarian summer rolls

1 package (14 ounces) firm tofu, drained

3½ ounces thin rice noodles (rice vermicelli)

½ cup soy sauce, divided

2 tablespoons lime juice

1 tablespoon sugar

2 cloves garlic, crushed

1 teaspoon rice vinegar

2 medium portobello mushrooms, cut into thin strips

1 teaspoon dark sesame oil

1 tablespoon vegetable oil

1 tablespoon sesame seeds

12 rice paper wrappers*

1 bunch fresh mint

½ cup shredded carrots

1 yellow bell pepper, cut into thin strips

* Rice paper is a thin, edible wrapper used in Southeast Asian cooking. It is available at well-stocked grocery stores or Asian markets.

1 Cut tofu crosswise into two pieces, each about 1 inch thick. Arrange between paper-towel lined cutting boards. Place weighted saucepan or baking dish on top; let stand 30 minutes to drain.

2 Place rice noodles in medium bowl; cover with hot water. Soak 20 to 30 minutes or until softened. Drain and cut into 3-inch lengths.

3 Meanwhile, prepare dipping sauce. Combine ¼ cup soy sauce, lime juice, sugar, garlic and vinegar in small bowl; stir until sugar is dissolved. Set aside.

4 Cut tofu into narrow strips about ¼ inch thick. Place in medium bowl with mushrooms. Add remaining ¼ cup soy sauce and sesame oil; toss gently. Heat vegetable oil in large skillet over medium heat. Add tofu and mushrooms; cook and stir until browned. Sprinkle with sesame seeds.

5 Soften rice paper wrappers, one at a time, in bowl of warm water 20 to 30 seconds. Remove to flat surface lined with dish towel. Arrange mint leaves in center of wrapper. Layer with tofu, mushroom, carrots, noodles and bell pepper.

6 Fold bottom of wrapper up over filling; fold in each side and roll up. Repeat with remaining wrappers. Wrap finished rolls individually in plastic wrap or cover with damp towel until ready to serve to prevent drying out. Serve with dipping sauce.

Makes 12 summer rolls

creamy cashew spread

1 cup raw cashews

2 tablespoons lemon juice

1 tablespoon tahini

½ teaspoon salt

½ teaspoon black pepper

2 teaspoons minced fresh herbs, such as basil, parsley or oregano (optional)

 1 Rinse cashews; place in medium bowl. Cover with water by at least 2 inches. Soak 4 hours or overnight.

2 Drain cashews, reserving soaking water. Combine cashews, lemon juice, tahini, salt, pepper and 2 tablespoons soaking water in food processor; process 4 to 6 minutes or until smooth. Add additional water if needed to achieve desired texture.

3 Refrigerate until ready to serve. Stir in herbs, if desired, just before serving.

Makes about ½ cup

TIP: Use as a spread or dip for hors d'oeuvres, or as a sandwich spread or pasta topping. Thin with additional liquid as needed.

beans and greens crostini

4 tablespoons olive oil, divided

1 small onion, thinly sliced

4 cups thinly sliced Italian black kale or other dinosaur kale variety

2 tablespoons minced garlic, divided

1 tablespoon balsamic vinegar

2 teaspoons salt, divided

¼ teaspoon red pepper flakes

1 can (about 15 ounces) cannellini beans, rinsed and drained

1 tablespoon chopped fresh rosemary

Toasted baguette slices

1 Heat 1 tablespoon oil in large nonstick skillet over medium heat. Add onion; cook and stir 5 minutes or until softened. Add kale and 1 tablespoon garlic; cook and stir 15 minutes or until kale is softened and most of liquid has evaporated. Stir in balsamic vinegar, 1 teaspoon salt and red pepper flakes.

2 Meanwhile, combine beans, remaining 3 tablespoons olive oil, 1 tablespoon garlic, 1 teaspoon salt and rosemary in food processor; process until smooth.

3 Spread baguette slices with bean mixture; top with kale.

Makes about 24 crostini

beer batter tempura

1½ cups all-purpose flour

1½ cups Japanese beer, chilled

1 teaspoon salt

Dipping Sauce (recipe follows)

Vegetable oil for frying

½ pound green beans or asparagus tips

1 large sweet potato, peeled and cut into ¼-inch slices

1 medium eggplant, cut into ¼-inch slices

1 Combine flour, beer and salt in medium bowl just until mixed. Batter should be thin and lumpy. *Do not overmix.* Let stand 15 minutes. Meanwhile, prepare Dipping Sauce.

2 Heat 1 inch of oil in large saucepan to 375°F; adjust heat to maintain temperature.

3 Dip 10 to 12 green beans in batter; add to hot oil. Fry until light golden brown. Remove to wire racks or paper towels to drain; keep warm. Repeat with remaining vegetables, working with only one vegetable at a time and being careful not to crowd vegetables. Serve with Dipping Sauce.

Makes 4 servings

dipping sauce

½ cup soy sauce

2 tablespoons rice wine

1 tablespoon sugar

½ teaspoon white vinegar

2 teaspoons minced fresh ginger

1 clove garlic, minced

2 green onions, thinly sliced

Combine soy sauce, rice wine, sugar and vinegar in small saucepan; cook and stir over medium heat 3 minutes or until sugar dissolves. Add ginger and garlic; cook and stir 2 minutes. Stir in green onions; remove from heat.

Makes about 1 cup

roasted eggplant spread

1 eggplant (1 pound)

1 medium tomato

1 tablespoon lemon juice

1 tablespoon chopped fresh basil *or* 1 teaspoon dried basil

2 teaspoons chopped fresh thyme *or* ¾ teaspoon dried thyme

1 clove garlic, minced

¼ teaspoon salt

1 tablespoon extra virgin olive oil

Focaccia or pita bread

1 Preheat oven to 400°F.

2 Pierce eggplant with fork in several places. Place on oven rack; bake 10 minutes. Cut off stem from tomato; place in small baking pan. Place tomato in oven with eggplant. Roast eggplant and tomato 40 minutes. Cool vegetables slightly. When cool enough to handle, peel eggplant and tomato. Coarsely chop eggplant.

3 Combine, eggplant, tomato, lemon juice, basil, thyme, garlic and salt in food processor; process until well blended. With motor running, slowly add oil and process until well blended. Refrigerate 3 hours or overnight.

4 Serve spread with focaccia.

Makes 10 servings

almond butter

1 package (16 ounces) lightly salted roasted almonds

2 tablespoons agave nectar

1½ tablespoons canola oil

Crackers or apple slices (optional)

1 Grate almonds in food processor using grating disk. Transfer almonds to large bowl. Remove grating disk; fit with metal blade.

2 Return almonds to food processor; process 2 to 3 minutes or until nuts clump together and form thick paste, scraping side of bowl occasionally. Add agave and oil; process until desired consistency is reached. Serve with crackers or apple slices, if desired. Store spread in airtight container in refrigerator.

Makes 1½ cups

roasted eggplant spread

scallion pancakes

2¼ cups all-purpose flour, divided

1 teaspoon sugar

⅔ cup boiling water

¼ to ½ cup cold water

2 teaspoons dark sesame oil

½ cup finely chopped green onion tops

1 teaspoon coarse salt

½ to ¾ cup vegetable oil

1 Combine 2 cups flour and sugar in large bowl. Stir in boiling water; mix with chopsticks or fork just until water is absorbed and mixture forms large clumps. Gradually stir in enough cold water until dough forms a ball and is no longer sticky.

2 Place dough on lightly floured surface; flatten slightly. Knead dough 5 minutes or until smooth and elastic. Wrap dough with plastic wrap; let stand 1 hour.

3 Unwrap dough and knead briefly on lightly floured surface; divide dough into four pieces. Roll one piece into 6- to 7-inch round, keeping remaining pieces wrapped in plastic wrap to prevent drying out. Brush dough with ½ teaspoon sesame oil; sprinkle evenly with 2 tablespoons green onions and ¼ teaspoon salt. Roll up jelly-roll style into tight cylinder.

4 Coil cylinder into a spiral and pinch end under into dough. Repeat with remaining dough pieces, sesame oil, green onions and salt. Cover with plastic wrap and let stand 15 minutes.

5 Roll each coiled piece of dough into 6- to 7-inch round on lightly floured surface with floured rolling pin.

6 Heat ½ cup vegetable oil in wok over medium-high heat to 375°F. Carefully place one pancake into hot oil. Fry 2 to 3 minutes per side or until golden. While pancake is frying, press center lightly with metal spatula to ensure even cooking. Remove to paper towels to drain. Repeat with remaining pancakes, adding additional oil if necessary and reheating oil between batches.

7 Cut each pancake into 8 wedges. Arrange on serving platter. Serve immediately.

Makes 32 wedges

SOUPS & STEWS

hot and sour soup with bok choy and tofu

1 tablespoon dark sesame oil

4 ounces fresh shiitake mushrooms, stems finely chopped, caps thinly sliced

2 cloves garlic, minced

2 cups mushroom broth or vegetable broth

1 cup plus 2 tablespoons cold water, divided

2 tablespoons reduced-sodium soy sauce

1½ tablespoons rice vinegar or white wine vinegar

¼ teaspoon red pepper flakes

1½ tablespoons cornstarch

2 cups coarsely chopped bok choy leaves or napa cabbage

10 ounces silken extra firm tofu, well drained, cut into ½-inch cubes

1 green onion, thinly sliced

1 Heat oil in large saucepan over medium heat. Add mushrooms and garlic; cook and stir 3 minutes. Add broth, 1 cup water, soy sauce, vinegar and red pepper flakes; bring to a boil. Reduce heat to low; simmer 5 minutes.

2 Whisk remaining 2 tablespoons water into cornstarch in small bowl until smooth. Stir into soup; simmer 2 minutes or until thickened. Stir in bok choy; simmer 2 to 3 minutes or until wilted. Stir in tofu; heat through. Ladle soup into bowls; sprinkle with green onion.

Makes 4 servings

middle eastern vegetable stew

¼ cup olive oil

3 cups (12 ounces) sliced zucchini

2 cups (6 ounces) cubed peeled eggplant

2 cups sliced quartered peeled sweet potatoes

1½ cups cubed peeled butternut squash (optional)

1 can (28 ounces) crushed tomatoes in purée

1 cup drained canned chickpeas

½ cup raisins or currants (optional)

1½ teaspoons ground cinnamon

1 teaspoon grated orange peel

¾ teaspoon ground cumin

½ teaspoon salt

½ teaspoon paprika

¼ to ½ teaspoon ground red pepper

⅛ teaspoon ground cardamom

Hot cooked whole wheat couscous or brown rice (optional)

1 Heat oil in large saucepan or Dutch oven over medium heat. Add zucchini, eggplant, sweet potatoes and squash, if desired; cook and stir 8 to 10 minutes or until vegetables are slightly softened.

2 Stir in tomatoes, chickpeas, raisins, if desired, cinnamon, orange peel, cumin, salt, paprika, ground red pepper and cardamom; bring to a boil over high heat. Reduce heat to low; cover and simmer 30 minutes or until vegetables are tender. If sauce becomes too thick, stir in water to thin. Serve over couscous, if desired.

Makes 6 servings

tex-mex black bean and corn stew

1 tablespoon canola or vegetable oil

1 small onion, chopped

4 cloves garlic, minced

1 teaspoon chili powder

1 teaspoon ground cumin

1 can (about **14** ounces) fire-roasted diced tomatoes

¾ cup salsa

2 medium zucchini or yellow squash (or **1** of each), cut into ½-inch pieces

1 can (about **15** ounces) black beans, rinsed and drained

1 cup frozen corn

¼ cup chopped fresh cilantro or green onions (optional)

1 Heat oil in large saucepan over medium heat. Add onion; cook and stir 5 minutes. Add garlic, chili powder and cumin; cook and stir 1 minute.

2 Stir in tomatoes, salsa, zucchini, beans and corn; bring to a boil over high heat. Reduce heat to low; cover and simmer 20 minutes or until vegetables are tender. Ladle into bowls; sprinkle with cilantro, if desired.

Makes 4 servings

curried parsnip soup

3 pounds parsnips, peeled and cut into 2-inch pieces

3 tablespoons olive oil, divided

1 medium yellow onion, chopped

2 stalks celery, diced

3 cloves garlic, minced

1 tablespoon salt

1 to 2 teaspoons curry powder

½ teaspoon grated fresh ginger

½ teaspoon black pepper

8 cups vegetable broth

Toasted bread slices (optional)

Chopped fresh chives (optional)

1 Preheat oven to 400°F. Line large baking sheet with foil.

2 Combine parsnips and 1 tablespoon oil in large bowl; toss to coat. Spread in single layer on prepared baking sheet. Bake 35 to 45 minutes or until parsnips are tender and lightly browned around edges, stirring once halfway through cooking.

3 Heat remaining 2 tablespoons oil in large saucepan or Dutch oven over medium heat. Add onion and celery; cook and stir about 8 minutes or until vegetables are tender and onion is translucent. Add garlic, salt, curry powder, ginger and pepper; cook and stir 1 minute. Add parsnips and broth; bring to a boil over medium-high heat. Reduce heat to medium-low; cover and simmer 10 minutes.

4 Working in batches, purée soup in blender or food processor. Transfer blended soup to large bowl. Serve with toasted bread, if desired; garnish with chives.

Makes 6 to 8 servings

cuban-style black bean soup

1 tablespoon olive oil

1 small onion, chopped

1 cup thinly sliced carrots

2 jalapeño peppers,* seeded and minced

2 cloves garlic, minced

1 can (about 15 ounces) black beans, undrained

1 can (about 14 ounces) vegetable broth

¼ cup chopped fresh cilantro

4 lime wedges (optional)

*Jalapeño peppers can sting and irritate the skin, so wear rubber gloves when handling peppers and do not touch your eyes.

1 Heat oil in large saucepan over medium heat. Add onion, carrots, jalapeños and garlic; cook and stir 5 minutes.

2 Add beans and broth; bring to a boil. Reduce heat to low; cover and simmer 15 to 20 minutes or until vegetables are very tender.

3 Ladle soup into bowls; sprinkle with cilantro and serve with lime wedges, if desired.

Makes 4 servings

NOTE: If desired, purée soup in a food processor or blender until smooth.

summer's best gazpacho

3 cups tomato juice

2½ cups finely diced tomatoes (2 large)

1 cup finely diced yellow or red bell pepper (1 small)

1 cup finely diced unpeeled cucumber

½ cup chunky salsa

1 tablespoon olive oil

1 clove garlic, minced

1 ripe avocado, diced

¼ cup finely chopped fresh cilantro or basil

 Combine tomato juice, tomatoes, bell pepper, cucumber, salsa, oil and garlic in large bowl; mix well. Cover and refrigerate at least 1 hour or up to 24 hours before serving.

2 Top with avocado and cilantro just before serving.

Makes 6 servings

smoky vegetable bean soup

2 tablespoons olive oil

1 medium red, yellow or orange bell pepper, chopped

1 clove garlic, minced

2 cups water

1 can (about 14 ounces) diced tomatoes

1 medium zucchini, thinly sliced lengthwise

⅛ teaspoon red pepper flakes

1 can (about 15 ounces) navy beans, rinsed and drained

3 to 4 tablespoons chopped fresh basil

1 tablespoon balsamic vinegar

¾ teaspoon salt

½ teaspoon liquid smoke (optional)

 Heat oil in large saucepan or Dutch oven over medium-high heat. Add bell pepper; cook and stir 4 minutes or until edges are browned. Add garlic; cook and stir 15 seconds. Add water, tomatoes, zucchini and red pepper flakes; bring to a boil over high heat. Reduce heat to low; cover and simmer 20 minutes.

2 Add beans, basil, vinegar, salt and liquid smoke, if desired; simmer 5 minutes.

Makes 4 servings

slow cooker veggie stew

1 tablespoon vegetable oil

⅔ cup carrot slices

½ cup diced onion

2 cloves garlic, chopped

2 cans (about 14 ounces each) vegetable broth

1½ cups chopped green cabbage

½ cup cut green beans

½ cup diced zucchini

1 tablespoon tomato paste

½ teaspoon dried basil

½ teaspoon dried oregano

¼ teaspoon salt

Slow Cooker Directions

1 Heat oil in medium skillet over medium-high heat. Add carrot, onion and garlic; cook and stir about 6 minutes or until tender. Transfer to slow cooker.

2 Stir in remaining ingredients. Cover; cook on LOW 8 to 10 hours or on HIGH 4 to 5 hours.

Makes 4 to 6 servings

moroccan lentil & vegetable soup

1 tablespoon olive oil

1 cup chopped onion

4 cloves garlic, minced

½ cup dried lentils, rinsed and sorted

1½ teaspoons ground coriander

1½ teaspoons ground cumin

½ teaspoon ground cinnamon

½ teaspoon black pepper

3¾ cups vegetable broth

½ cup chopped celery

½ cup chopped sun-dried tomatoes (not packed in oil)

1 yellow squash, chopped

½ cup chopped green bell pepper

1 cup chopped plum tomatoes

½ cup chopped fresh Italian parsley

¼ cup chopped fresh cilantro or basil

1 Heat oil in large saucepan or Dutch oven over medium-high heat. Add onion and garlic; cook and stir 4 minutes or until onion is tender. Stir in lentils, coriander, cumin, cinnamon and black pepper; cook 2 minutes. Add broth, celery and sun-dried tomatoes; bring to a boil. Reduce heat to medium-low; cover and simmer 25 minutes.

2 Stir in squash and bell pepper; cover and simmer 10 minutes or until lentils are tender.

3 Top with plum tomatoes, parsley and cilantro just before serving.

Makes 6 servings

TIP: Many soups, including this one, taste even better the next day after the flavors have had time to blend. Cover and refrigerate the soup overnight, reserving the plum tomatoes, parsley and cilantro until ready to serve.

miso soup with tofu

4 cups water

1 tablespoon shredded nori or wakame seaweed

7 ounces firm tofu

3 green onions, finely chopped

¼ cup white miso

2 teaspoons soy sauce

1 Bring water to a simmer in medium saucepan over medium-low heat. Add nori; simmer 6 minutes.

2 Meanwhile, press tofu between paper towels to remove excess water. Cut into ½-inch cubes.

3 Reduce heat to low. Add tofu, green onions, miso and soy sauce; cook and stir until miso is dissolved and soup is heated through. *Do not boil.*

Makes 4 servings

spring vegetable ragoût

1 tablespoon olive oil

2 leeks, thinly sliced

3 cloves garlic, minced

1 package (10 ounces) frozen corn

1 cup vegetable broth

8 ounces yellow squash, halved lengthwise and cut into ½-inch pieces (about 1¼ cups)

6 ounces frozen shelled edamame

1 small package (4 ounces) shredded carrots

3 cups small cherry tomatoes, halved

1 teaspoon dried tarragon

1 teaspoon dried basil

1 teaspoon dried oregano

Salt and black pepper

Minced fresh parsley (optional)

1 Heat oil in large skillet over medium heat. Add leeks and garlic; cook and stir just until fragrant. Add corn, broth, squash, edamame and carrots; cook and stir about 6 minutes or until squash is tender.

2 Stir in tomatoes, tarragon, basil and oregano; cover and simmer over low heat 2 minutes or until tomatoes are soft. Season with salt and pepper. Garnish with parsley.

Makes 6 servings

italian escarole and white bean stew

1 tablespoon olive oil

1 onion, chopped

3 carrots, cut into ½-inch slices

2 cloves garlic, minced

1 can (about 14 ounces) vegetable broth

1 head escarole (about 12 ounces)

¼ teaspoon red pepper flakes

2 cans (about 15 ounces each) Great Northern beans, rinsed and drained

Salt

Vegan Parmesan-flavor topping (optional)

Slow Cooker Directions

1 Heat oil in medium skillet over medium-high heat. Add onion and carrots; cook and stir about 5 minutes or until onion is softened. Add garlic; cook and stir 1 minute. Transfer to slow cooker. Pour in broth.

2 Trim base of escarole. Roughly cut crosswise into 1-inch-wide strips. Wash well in large bowl of cold water. Lift out by handfuls, leaving sand or dirt in bottom of bowl. Shake to remove excess water but do not dry. Add to slow cooker. Sprinkle with red pepper flakes; top with beans.

3 Cover; cook on LOW 7 to 8 hours or on HIGH 3½ to 4 hours or until escarole is wilted and very tender. Season with salt. Ladle into bowls and sprinkle with Parmesan-flavor topping, if desired.

Makes 4 servings

NOTE: Escarole is very leafy and easily fills a 4½-quart slow cooker when raw, but it shrinks dramatically as it cooks down.

zesty chili

1 tablespoon canola or vegetable oil

1 large red bell pepper, coarsely chopped

2 medium zucchini or yellow squash (or 1 of each), cut into ½-inch pieces

4 cloves garlic, minced

1 can (about 14 ounces) fire-roasted diced tomatoes

¾ cup chunky salsa

2 teaspoons chili powder

1 teaspoon dried oregano

1 can (about 15 ounces) red kidney beans, rinsed and drained

10 ounces extra firm tofu, well drained and cut into ½-inch cubes

Chopped fresh cilantro (optional)

1 Heat oil in large saucepan over medium heat. Add bell pepper; cook and stir 4 minutes. Add zucchini and garlic; cook and stir 3 minutes.

2 Stir in tomatoes, salsa, chili powder and oregano; bring to a boil over high heat. Reduce heat to low; simmer 15 minutes or until vegetables are tender.

3 Stir in beans; simmer 2 minutes or until heated through. Stir in tofu; remove from heat. Ladle into bowls; sprinkle with cilantro, if desired.

Makes 4 servings

chilled cucumber soup

1 large cucumber, peeled and coarsely chopped

¾ cup silken tofu or dairy-free sour cream

¼ cup packed fresh dill

½ teaspoon salt

⅛ teaspoon ground white pepper

1½ cups vegetable broth

Dill sprigs

1 Place cucumber in food processor; process until finely chopped. Add tofu, ¼ cup dill, salt and pepper; process until almost smooth.

2 Transfer mixture to large bowl; stir in broth. Cover and refrigerate at least 2 hours or up to 24 hours. Ladle into bowls; garnish with dill sprigs.

Makes 4 servings

SANDWICHES & WRAPS

portobello mushroom burgers

1 tablespoon olive oil, divided

¾ cup thinly sliced shallots

½ cup vegan mayonnaise

¼ cup chopped fresh basil

4 large portobello mushrooms, washed, patted dry and stems removed

⅛ teaspoon salt

⅛ teaspoon black pepper

2 cloves garlic, minced

4 whole grain hamburger buns

4 ounces dairy-free mozzarella cheese alternative, cut into ¼-inch slices (optional)

2 jarred roasted red bell peppers, rinsed, patted dry and cut into strips

1 Heat 1 teaspoon oil in medium saucepan over medium heat. Add shallots; cook and stir 6 to 8 minutes or until golden brown and soft. Combine mayonnaise and basil in small bowl; set aside.

2 Preheat broiler. Line baking sheet with foil. Drizzle both sides of mushrooms with remaining 2 teaspoons oil; season with salt and black pepper.

3 Place mushrooms, cap sides down, on prepared baking sheet. Sprinkle with garlic. Broil mushrooms 8 minutes, turning once.

4 Spread mayonnaise mixture on cut sides of buns. Serve dairy-free mozzarella, if desired, shallots, mushrooms and roasted peppers on buns.

Makes 4 servings

ginger-soy grilled tofu sandwiches

2 tablespoons reduced-sodium soy sauce

1 tablespoon dark sesame oil

1 clove garlic, minced

1 teaspoon minced fresh ginger

¼ teaspoon red pepper flakes

1 package (14 ounces) extra firm tofu, well drained

1 large red or yellow bell pepper, quartered lengthwise

1½ cups packed mixed salad greens

1 baguette (8 ounces), cut crosswise into 4 pieces and split

1 Spray grill basket, grill pan or grid with nonstick cooking spray. Prepare grill for direct cooking. Combine soy sauce, oil, garlic, ginger and red pepper flakes in small bowl; mix well. Place 1 tablespoon mixture in medium bowl; set aside.

2 Pat tofu dry with paper towel. Cut tofu crosswise into 4 slices; place in shallow baking dish. Spoon remaining soy sauce mixture over tofu; turn to coat.

3 Place bell pepper in grill basket; grill, uncovered, over medium-high heat 4 minutes. Turn bell pepper and add tofu to grill; grill 4 minutes. Turn pepper and tofu; brush tofu with any remaining soy sauce from dish. Grill 3 to 4 minutes or until tofu is browned and pepper is tender.

4 Add salad greens to reserved soy sauce mixture; toss to coat. Serve greens, bell pepper and tofu on baguettes.

Makes 4 servings

bean and vegetable burritos

2 tablespoons chili powder

2 teaspoons dried oregano

1½ teaspoons ground cumin

1 large sweet potato, peeled and diced

1 can (about 15 ounces) black or pinto beans, rinsed and drained

4 cloves garlic, minced

1 medium onion, halved and thinly sliced

1 jalapeño pepper, seeded and minced*

1 green bell pepper, chopped

1 cup frozen corn, thawed and drained

3 tablespoons lime juice

1 tablespoon chopped fresh cilantro

¾ cup (3 ounces) shredded dairy-free cheese alternative

4 (10-inch) flour tortillas

*Jalapeño peppers can sting and irritate the skin, so wear rubber gloves when handling peppers and do not touch your eyes.

Slow Cooker Directions

1 Combine chili powder, oregano and cumin in small bowl.

2 Layer ingredients in slow cooker in following order: sweet potato, beans, half of chili powder mixture, garlic, onion, jalapeño, bell pepper, remaining half of chili powder mixture and corn. Cover; cook on LOW 5 hours or until sweet potato is tender. Stir in lime juice and cilantro.

3 Preheat oven to 350°F. Spoon 2 tablespoons dairy-free cheese in center of each tortilla; top with 1 cup filling. Fold two sides over filling and roll up. Place burritos, seam side down, on baking sheet. Cover with foil and bake 20 to 30 minutes or until heated through.

Makes 4 servings

tip

Once you've added the ingredients to the slow cooker, keep the lid on! The slow cooker can take as long as 30 minutes to regain heat lost when the cover is removed. Only remove the cover when instructed to do so by the recipe.

farro veggie burgers

1½ cups water

½ cup pearled farro or spelt

2 medium potatoes, peeled and quartered

2 to 4 tablespoons canola oil, divided

¾ cup finely chopped green onions

1 cup grated carrots

2 teaspoons grated fresh ginger

2 tablespoons ground almonds

¼ to ¾ teaspoon salt

¼ teaspoon black pepper

½ cup panko bread crumbs

6 whole wheat hamburger buns

Ketchup and mustard (optional)

1 Combine 1½ cups water and farro in medium saucepan; bring to a boil over high heat. Reduce heat to low; partially cover and cook 25 to 30 minutes or until farro is tender. Drain and cool. (If using spelt, use 2 cups of water and cook until tender.)

2 Meanwhile, place potatoes in large saucepan; cover with water. Bring to a boil; reduce heat and simmer 20 minutes or until tender. Cool and mash potatoes; set aside.

3 Heat 1 tablespoon oil in medium skillet over medium-high heat. Add green onions; cook and stir 1 minute. Add carrots and ginger; cover and cook 2 to 3 minutes or until carrots are tender. Transfer to large bowl; cool completely.

4 Add mashed potatoes and farro to carrot mixture. Add almonds, salt and pepper; mix well. Shape mixture into six patties. Spread panko on medium plate; coat patties with panko.

5 Heat 1 tablespoon oil in large nonstick skillet over medium heat. Cook patties about 8 minutes or until golden brown, turning once and adding additional oil as needed. Serve on buns with desired condiments.

Makes 6 servings

NOTE: Farro is a whole grain and belongs to the wheat family. It's very close to spelt, and it is rich in fiber, magnesium and vitamins A, B, C, and E. Farro has a nutty flavor and a chewy bite. It can be used in place of rice in many dishes.

eggless egg salad sandwich

1 package (14 ounces) firm tofu, drained, pressed* and crumbled

1 stalk celery, finely diced

2 green onions, minced

2 tablespoons minced parsley

¼ cup plus 1 tablespoon vegan mayonnaise

3 tablespoons sweet pickle relish

2 teaspoons fresh lemon juice

1 teaspoon mustard

Black pepper

8 slices whole wheat bread, toasted

1 cup alfalfa sprouts

8 tomato slices

*Cut tofu in half horizontally and place it between layers of paper towels. Place a weighted cutting board on top; let stand 15 to 30 minutes.

1 Combine tofu, celery, green onions and parsley in large bowl. Whisk mayonnaise, relish, lemon juice, mustard and pepper in small bowl until well blended. Add to tofu mixture; mix well.

2 Serve salad on toast with alfalfa sprouts and tomato slices.

Makes 4 servings

mediterranean vegetable sandwiches

1 small eggplant, peeled, halved and cut into ¼-inch-thick slices

Salt

1 small zucchini, halved and cut lengthwise into ¼-inch-thick slices

1 red bell pepper, sliced

3 tablespoons balsamic vinegar

½ teaspoon garlic powder

2 French bread rolls, cut in half horizontally

1 Place eggplant in non-aluminum colander; lightly sprinkle with salt. Let stand 30 minutes. Rinse eggplant; pat dry with paper towels.

2 Preheat broiler. Spray rack with nonstick cooking spray. Place vegetables on rack. Broil 4 inches from heat source 8 to 10 minutes or until vegetables are browned, turning once.

3 Whisk vinegar and garlic powder in medium bowl until well blended. Add vegetables; toss to coat evenly. Serve immediately on rolls.

Makes 2 servings

grilled vegetable and hummus muffaletta

1 small eggplant, cut lengthwise into ⅛-inch slices

1 yellow squash, cut lengthwise into ⅛-inch slices

1 zucchini, cut diagonally into ⅛-inch slices

¼ cup extra virgin olive oil

½ teaspoon salt

¼ teaspoon black pepper

1 (8-inch) boule or round bread, cut in half horizontally

1 container (8 ounces) hummus, any flavor

1 jar (12 ounces) roasted red bell peppers, drained

1 jar (6 ounces) marinated artichoke hearts, drained and chopped

1 small tomato, thinly sliced

1 Preheat grill or grill pan. Combine eggplant, squash, zucchini, oil, salt and pepper in large bowl; toss to coat.

2 Grill vegetables 2 to 3 minutes per side or until tender and golden. Cool to room temperature.

3 Scoop out bread from both halves of boule with fingers, leaving about 1 inch of bread on edges and about 1½ inches on bottom. (Reserve bread for bread crumbs or croutons.) Spread hummus evenly on bottom half of bread.

4 Layer grilled vegetables, roasted peppers, artichokes and tomato over hummus; cover with top half of bread. Wrap stuffed loaf tightly in plastic wrap. Refrigerate at least 1 hour before cutting into wedges.

Makes 6 servings

vegan sloppy joes

2 cups textured soy protein (TVP)

1¾ cups boiling water

½ cup ketchup

½ cup barbecue sauce

2 tablespoons cider vinegar

1 tablespoon packed brown sugar

1 tablespoon soy sauce

1 teaspoon chili powder

1 tablespoon olive oil

½ cup chopped onion

½ cup chopped carrot

¾ cup water

4 to 6 hamburger buns

1 Combine TVP and boiling water in large bowl; let stand 10 minutes.

2 For sauce, combine ketchup, barbecue sauce, vinegar, brown sugar, soy sauce and chili powder in medium bowl; mix well.

3 Heat oil in large saucepan over medium-high heat. Add onion and carrot; cook and stir 5 minutes or until vegetables are tender. Stir in sauce mixture; bring to a boil. Stir in reconstituted TVP and ¾ cup water. Reduce heat to low; cover and cook 20 minutes. Serve sloppy joes in buns.

Makes 4 to 6 servings

mustard glazed tofu burgers

1 package (14 ounces) extra firm tofu, pressed*

2 to 3 tablespoons chopped fresh basil

2 to 3 tablespoons honey mustard

2 teaspoons olive oil

2 cloves garlic, minced

4 multigrain sandwich rounds, split and lightly toasted

½ cup packed arugula or watercress

8 thin slices ripe tomato

*Cut tofu in half horizontally; cut in half crosswise to make four rectangles. Place tofu between layers of paper towels. Place a weighted cutting board on top; let stand 15 to 30 minutes.

1 Oil grid; prepare grill for direct cooking.

2 Combine basil, mustard, oil and garlic in small bowl; mix well. Spread half of mixture over tofu.

3 Place tofu slices on grid, mustard side down. Spread remaining mustard mixture over tofu. Grill, covered, over medium heat 8 minutes or until browned, turning once.

4 Serve on sandwich rounds with arugula and tomato slices.

Makes 4 servings

black bean and tempeh wraps

2 teaspoons olive oil

½ cup chopped onion

½ cup chopped green bell pepper

2 cloves garlic, minced

2 teaspoons chili powder

2 cans (about 14 ounces each) stewed tomatoes

1 teaspoon dried oregano

½ teaspoon dried coriander

1 can (about 15 ounces) black beans, rinsed and drained

4 ounces tempeh, diced

¼ cup minced onion

¼ teaspoon black pepper

½ teaspoon ground cumin

8 (6-inch) flour tortillas

1 For sauce, heat oil in large nonstick skillet over medium heat. Add chopped onion, bell pepper and garlic; cook and stir 5 minutes or until onion is tender. Add chili powder; cook and stir 1 minute. Add tomatoes, oregano and coriander; cook 15 minutes, stirring frequently.

2 Preheat oven to 350°F. Spray 13×9-inch baking dish with nonstick cooking spray. Place beans in medium bowl; mash well with fork. Stir in tempeh, minced onion, black pepper and cumin. Stir in ¼ cup sauce.

3 Soften tortillas if necessary.* Spread ⅓ cup bean mixture down center of each tortilla. Roll up tortillas; place in single layer in shallow baking dish. Top with remaining sauce.

4 Bake 15 minutes or until heated through.

Makes 4 servings

To soften tortillas, wrap stack of tortillas in foil. Heat in preheated 350°F oven about 10 minutes or until softened.

middle eastern grilled vegetable wraps

1 medium red bell pepper,
    cut into quarters

1 medium green bell pepper,
    cut into quarters

1 large eggplant (about
    1 pound), cut crosswise
    into ¼-inch slices

12 ounces large fresh
    mushrooms

2 green onions, sliced

¼ cup fresh lemon juice

⅛ teaspoon black pepper

4 (10-inch) flour tortillas

½ cup (4 ounces) hummus

⅓ cup lightly packed fresh
    cilantro

12 large fresh basil leaves

12 large fresh mint leaves

1 Prepare grill for direct cooking.

2 Grill bell peppers, skin side down, over high heat until skins are blackened. Place in paper bag; close bag. Let stand 5 to 10 minutes or until cool enough to handle. Peel peppers.

3 Lightly spray eggplant with cooking spray. Thread mushrooms onto metal skewers. Grill eggplant and mushrooms, covered, over medium heat about 4 minutes or until tender and lightly browned, turning once.

4 Cut eggplant and bell peppers into ½-inch strips; cut mushrooms into quarters. Combine vegetables, green onions, lemon juice and black pepper in medium bowl.

5 Grill tortillas about 1 minute or until warm, turning once. Spoon 2 tablespoons hummus down center of each tortilla. Top with one fourth of cilantro, 3 basil leaves, 3 mint leaves and one fourth of vegetables. Roll to enclose filling; serve immediately.

Makes 4 servings

crunchy vegetable pita pockets

2 tablespoons lime juice

2 teaspoons natural peanut butter

2 teaspoons agave nectar

2 teaspoons reduced-sodium soy sauce

½ teaspoon hot pepper sauce (optional)

1 cup shredded red cabbage

1 cup red bell pepper slices

½ cup frozen shelled edamame, thawed

1 whole wheat pita bread round, cut in half and lightly toasted

1 Whisk lime juice, peanut butter, agave, soy sauce and hot pepper sauce, if desired, in medium bowl until smooth and well blended. Add cabbage, bell pepper and edamame; stir to coat.

2 Serve vegetable mixture in pita bread.

Makes 2 servings

PASTA & NOODLES

summer spaghetti

1 pound plum tomatoes, coarsely chopped

1 medium onion, chopped

6 pitted green olives, chopped

⅓ cup chopped fresh parsley

2 tablespoons finely shredded fresh basil _or_ ¾ teaspoon dried basil

2 cloves garlic, minced

2 teaspoons drained capers

½ teaspoon paprika

¼ teaspoon dried oregano

1 tablespoon red wine vinegar

½ cup olive oil

1 pound uncooked spaghetti

1 Combine tomatoes, onion, olives, parsley, basil, garlic, capers, paprika and oregano in medium bowl; mix well. Drizzle with vinegar. Add oil; stir until well blended. Cover and refrigerate at least 6 hours or overnight.

2 Cook spaghetti according to package directions; drain. Toss hot pasta with tomato mixture. Serve immediately.

**Makes 4 to 6 servings**

vegan artichoke lasagna

1 tablespoon olive oil

1 cup chopped onion

3 cloves garlic, chopped

¼ cup tomato paste

¼ cup white wine

1 can (28 ounces) Italian plum tomatoes, undrained, or crushed tomatoes

1 teaspoon coarse salt

1 teaspoon sugar

1 teaspoon dried oregano

9 uncooked lasagna noodles

   Not-Ricotta (page 102)

1 can (14 ounces) artichoke hearts, drained and chopped

1 package (10 ounces) frozen chopped spinach, thawed and squeezed dry

2 cups (8 ounces) shredded dairy-free mozzarella cheese alternative

2 roasted bell peppers, chopped

1 For sauce, heat oil in large saucepan over medium-high heat. Add onion and garlic; cook and stir 5 minutes or until onion is tender. Stir in tomato paste; cook 1 minute. Stir in wine; cook 30 seconds. Add tomatoes with juice, salt, sugar and oregano; break up tomatoes with spoon. Reduce heat to low; cover and simmer 30 minutes.

2 Meanwhile, cook lasagna noodles according to package directions. Drain and return to saucepan; cover with cold water to prevent sticking.

3 Prepare Not-Ricotta. Combine artichokes and spinach in small bowl.

4 Preheat oven to 350°F. Spray 13×9-inch baking dish with nonstick cooking spray. Spread ½ cup sauce in bottom of dish; arrange three noodles over sauce. Spread half of Not-Ricotta over noodles; top with artichoke mixture, half of dairy-free mozzarella and ½ cup sauce. Repeat layers of noodles and Not-Ricotta; top with roasted peppers, remaining 3 noodles, sauce and dairy-free mozzarella.

5 Cover with greased foil; bake 45 minutes. Remove foil; bake 15 minutes. Let stand 10 minutes before serving.

Makes 8 servings

spicy sesame noodles

6 ounces uncooked soba (buckwheat) noodles

2 teaspoons dark sesame oil

1 tablespoon sesame seeds

½ cup vegetable broth

1 tablespoon creamy peanut butter

½ cup thinly sliced green onions

½ cup minced red bell pepper

4 teaspoons reduced-sodium soy sauce

1½ teaspoons finely chopped seeded jalapeño pepper*

1 clove garlic, minced

¼ teaspoon red pepper flakes

Jalapeño peppers can sting and irritate the skin, so wear rubber gloves when handling peppers and do not touch your eyes.

1 Cook soba noodles according to package directions. *Do not overcook.* Rinse noodles thoroughly under cold running water; drain. Place noodles in large bowl; toss with oil.

2 Cook sesame seeds in small skillet over medium heat about 3 minutes or until seeds begin to pop and turn golden brown, stirring frequently. Remove from skillet.

3 Whisk broth and peanut butter in medium bowl until blended. (Mixture may look curdled.) Stir in green onions, bell pepper, soy sauce, jalapeño, garlic and red pepper flakes.

4 Pour mixture over noodles; toss to coat. Cover and let stand at room temperature 30 minutes or refrigerate up to 24 hours. Sprinkle with toasted sesame seeds before serving.

Makes 4 servings

dairy-free mac and cheez

1½ cups uncooked elbow macaroni

1 cup chopped onion

1 cup chopped red or green bell pepper

¾ cup chopped celery

¾ cup nutritional yeast

¼ cup all-purpose flour

1½ teaspoons salt

¼ teaspoon garlic powder

¼ teaspoon onion powder

2 cups unsweetened soymilk or other dairy-free milk

1 teaspoon yellow mustard

3 drops hot pepper sauce (optional)

½ teaspoon paprika

1 Preheat oven to 350°F. Spray 13×9-inch baking dish with nonstick cooking spray. Cook macaroni according to package directions; add onion, bell pepper and celery during last 5 minutes of cooking. Drain and return to saucepan.

2 Meanwhile, combine nutritional yeast, flour, salt, garlic powder and onion powder in medium saucepan. Whisk in soymilk over medium heat until smooth. Add mustard and hot pepper sauce, if desired. Continue whisking 10 minutes or until mixture thickens to desired consistency. Pour over macaroni and vegetables; mix well.

3 Spread mixture in prepared baking dish; sprinkle with paprika. Bake 15 to 20 minutes or until heated through.

Makes 4 to 6 servings

TIP: Try this sauce over vegetables for a creamy side dish or over corn chips for nachos.

soba stir-fry

8 ounces uncooked soba (buckwheat) noodles

1 tablespoon olive oil

2 cups sliced shiitake mushrooms

1 medium red bell pepper, cut into thin strips

2 whole dried red chiles *or* ¼ teaspoon red pepper flakes

1 clove garlic, minced

2 cups shredded napa cabbage

½ cup reduced-sodium vegetable broth

2 tablespoons reduced-sodium tamari or soy sauce

1 tablespoon rice wine or dry sherry

2 teaspoons cornstarch

1 package (14 ounces) firm tofu, drained and cut into 1-inch cubes

2 green onions, thinly sliced

1 Cook soba noodles according to package directions. *Do not overcook.* Drain and set aside.

2 Heat oil in large nonstick skillet or wok over medium-high heat. Add mushrooms, bell pepper, dried chiles and garlic; stir-fry 3 minutes or until mushrooms are tender. Add cabbage; cover and cook 2 minutes or until cabbage is wilted.

3 Whisk broth, tamari and rice wine into cornstarch in small bowl until smooth. Stir sauce into vegetable mixture; cook 2 minutes or until sauce is thickened.

4 Stir in tofu and noodles; toss gently until heated through. Sprinkle with green onions. Serve immediately.

Makes 4 servings

quick szechuan vegetable lo mein

2 cans (about 14 ounces each) vegetable broth

2 teaspoons minced garlic

1 teaspoon minced fresh ginger

¼ teaspoon red pepper flakes

1 package (16 ounces) frozen vegetable medley, such as broccoli, carrots, water chestnuts and red bell peppers

1 package (5 ounces) Asian curly noodles or 5 ounces uncooked angel hair pasta, broken in half

3 tablespoons soy sauce

1 tablespoon dark sesame oil

¼ cup thinly sliced green onions

1 Combine broth, garlic, ginger and red pepper flakes in wok or large skillet; bring to a boil over high heat.

2 Add vegetables and noodles; cover and return to a boil. Reduce heat to medium-low; simmer, uncovered, 5 to 6 minutes or until vegetables and noodles are tender, stirring occasionally.

3 Stir in soy sauce and sesame oil; cook 3 minutes. Stir in green onions just before serving.

Makes 4 servings

NOTE: For a heartier, protein-packed main dish, add 1 package (14 ounces) extra firm tofu, drained and cut into ¾-inch cubes, to the broth mixture with the soy sauce and sesame oil.

tip

Making homemade vegetable broth is easy, and it's a great way to use up vegetables that are past their prime. Heat 1 tablespoon oil in a large saucepan or Dutch oven. Add onion wedges, unpeeled garlic cloves and coarsely chopped carrots and celery; cook and stir 5 minutes. Add 8 to 12 cups of water, fresh or dried herbs, whole peppercorns and salt; bring to a boil. Cover and simmer 30 minutes to 1 hour. Strain the broth and use immediately or store in airtight containers in the refrigerator for up to a week.

spinach fettuccine with garlic-onion sauce

¼ cup (½ stick) dairy-free margarine

2 tablespoons olive oil

1 pound Vidalia or other sweet onions, sliced

12 cloves garlic, chopped

1 tablespoon agave nectar

1 pound uncooked spinach fettuccine

¼ cup Marsala wine

Salt and black pepper

Vegan Parmesan-flavor topping (optional)

1 Heat margarine and oil in large skillet over medium heat. Add onions and garlic; cover and cook until soft. Add agave; cook, uncovered, over low heat 30 minutes, stirring occasionally.

2 Meanwhile, cook fettuccine according to package directions; drain and keep warm.

3 Stir Marsala into onion mixture; cook 5 to 10 minutes. Season with salt and pepper. Pour sauce over pasta; toss to coat. Sprinkle with Parmesan-flavor topping, if desired. Serve immediately.

Makes 4 servings

peanut-sauced pasta

⅓ cup vegetable broth

3 tablespoons creamy
   peanut butter

2 tablespoons seasoned
   rice vinegar

2 tablespoons reduced-
   sodium soy sauce

½ teaspoon red pepper flakes

9 ounces uncooked
   multigrain linguine

1½ pounds fresh asparagus,
   cut into 1-inch pieces
   (4 cups)

⅓ cup dry-roasted peanuts,
   chopped

1 Whisk broth, peanut butter, vinegar, soy sauce and red pepper flakes in small saucepan until smooth. Cook over low heat until heated through, stirring frequently. Keep warm.

2 Cook linguine according to package directions. Add asparagus during last 5 minutes of cooking. Drain pasta and asparagus; toss with peanut sauce. Sprinkle with peanuts.

Makes 4 servings

spicy manicotti

3 cups Not-Ricotta (recipe follows)

⅔ cup vegan Parmesan-flavor topping, plus additional for serving

2½ tablespoons chopped fresh parsley

1 teaspoon Italian seasoning

½ teaspoon garlic powder

½ teaspoon salt

½ teaspoon black pepper

12 ounces soy chorizo, meatless Italian sausage or soy crumbles

1 can (28 ounces) crushed tomatoes

1 jar (26 ounces) marinara sauce

8 ounces uncooked manicotti pasta shells

1 Preheat oven to 375°F. Spray 13×9-inch baking dish with nonstick cooking spray. Prepare Not Ricotta.

2 For filling, combine Not-Ricotta, ⅔ cup Parmesan-flavor topping, parsley, Italian seasoning, garlic powder, salt and pepper in medium bowl.

3 Crumble soy chorizo into large skillet; cook and stir over medium-high heat until browned. Remove from skillet; set aside.

4 Add tomatoes and marinara sauce to same skillet; bring to a boil over high heat. Reduce heat to low; simmer, uncovered, 10 minutes. Pour about one third of sauce into prepared dish.

5 Stuff each shell with about ½ cup filling; arrange filled shell in prepared baking dish. Top with sausage and remaining sauce.

6 Cover tightly with foil; bake 50 minutes to 1 hour or until pasta is tender. Let stand 5 minutes before serving. Sprinkle with additional Parmesan-flavor topping.

Makes 8 to 10 servings

not-ricotta

1 package (14 ounces) firm tofu, drained and pressed

1 cup silken tofu

½ cup chopped fresh parsley

2 teaspoons coarse salt

2 teaspoons lemon juice

1 teaspoon sugar

1 teaspoon black pepper

Crumble firm tofu into large bowl. Add silken tofu, parsley, salt, lemon juice, sugar and pepper; mix well. Refrigerate until needed. Drain liquid before using.

Makes 3 cups

lemon-tossed linguine

8 ounces uncooked linguine

3 tablespoons fresh lemon juice

1 tablespoon dairy-free margarine

2 tablespoons minced chives

⅓ cup dairy-free milk

1 teaspoon cornstarch

1 tablespoon minced fresh dill

1 tablespoon minced fresh parsley

2 teaspoons grated lemon peel

¼ teaspoon white pepper

3 tablespoons vegan Parmesan-flavor topping

Lemon slices and fresh dill sprigs (optional)

1 Cook linguine according to package directions; drain well. Place in medium bowl; sprinkle with lemon juice.

2 Meanwhile, melt margarine in small saucepan over medium heat. Add chives; cook and stir until softened.

3 Stir dairy-free milk into cornstarch in small bowl until smooth. Add to saucepan; cook and stir until thickened. Stir in dill, parsley, lemon peel and pepper.

4 Pour sauce over noodles. Sprinkle with Parmesan-flavor topping; toss to coat. Garnish with lemon slices and dill sprigs. Serve immediately.

Makes 2 servings

curried noodles

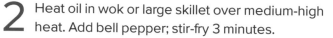

7 ounces thin rice noodles (rice vermicelli)

1 tablespoon peanut or vegetable oil

1 large red bell pepper, cut into short, thin strips

2 green onions, cut into ½-inch pieces

1 clove garlic, minced

1 teaspoon minced fresh ginger

2 teaspoons curry powder

⅛ to ¼ teaspoon red pepper flakes

½ cup vegetable broth

2 tablespoons soy sauce

1 Place noodles in large bowl; cover with boiling water. Let stand 15 minutes to soften. Drain and cut into 3-inch pieces.

2 Heat oil in wok or large skillet over medium-high heat. Add bell pepper; stir-fry 3 minutes.

3 Add green onions, garlic and ginger; stir-fry 1 minute. Add curry powder and red pepper flakes; stir-fry 1 minute.

4 Add broth and soy sauce; cook and stir 2 minutes. Add noodles; cook and stir 3 minutes or until heated through.

Makes 6 servings

penne pasta with chunky tomato sauce and spinach

8 ounces multigrain penne pasta

2 cups spicy marinara sauce

1 large ripe tomato, chopped (about 1½ cups)

4 cups packed baby spinach or torn spinach leaves (4 ounces)

¼ cup vegan Parmesan-flavor topping

¼ cup chopped fresh basil

1 Cook pasta according to package directions.

2 Meanwhile, heat marinara sauce and tomato in medium saucepan over medium heat 3 to 4 minutes or until hot and bubbly, stirring occasionally. Remove from heat; stir in spinach.

3 Drain pasta; return to saucepan. Add sauce; toss to coat. Sprinkle with Parmsan-flavor topping and basil.

Makes 4 to 6 servings

PROTEIN POWER

barbecue seitan skewers

1 package (8 ounces) seitan, cubed

½ cup barbecue sauce, divided

1 red bell pepper, cut into 12 pieces

1 green bell pepper, cut into 12 pieces

12 mushrooms

1 zucchini, cut into 12 pieces

1 Place seitan in medium bowl. Add ¼ cup barbecue sauce; stir to coat. Marinate in refrigerator 30 minutes. Soak four bamboo skewers in water 20 minutes.

2 Oil grid. Prepare grill for direct cooking. Thread seitan, bell peppers, mushrooms and zucchini onto skewers.

3 Grill skewers, covered, over medium-high heat 8 minutes or until seitan is hot and glazed with sauce, brushing with remaining sauce and turning occasionally.

Makes 4 servings

thai-style rice noodles

½ cup soy sauce

⅓ cup sugar

¼ cup lime juice

2 fresh red Thai chiles *or*
1 large jalapeño pepper,*
finely chopped

¼ cup vegetable oil

7 ounces firm tofu, drained
and cut into triangles

1 jicama (8 ounces), peeled
and chopped *or* 1 can
(8 ounces) sliced water
chestnuts, drained

2 medium sweet potatoes
(1 pound), peeled and cut
into ¼-inch-thick slices

2 large leeks, cut into
¼-inch-thick slices

8 ounces thin rice noodles
(rice vermicelli)

¼ cup chopped unsalted
dry-roasted peanuts

2 tablespoons chopped
fresh mint

2 tablespoons chopped
fresh cilantro

*Chile peppers can sting and irritate
the skin, so wear rubber gloves when
handling peppers and do not touch
your eyes.*

1 Whisk soy sauce, sugar, lime juice and chiles in small bowl until well blended.

2 Place rice noodles in medium bowl. Cover with hot water; let stand 15 minutes or until soft. Drain well; cut into 3-inch lengths.

3 Meanwhile, heat oil in large skillet over medium-high heat. Add tofu; cook 8 minutes or until golden, turning once. Remove with slotted spatula to paper towel-lined baking sheet.

4 Add jicama to skillet; stir-fry 5 minutes or until lightly browned. Remove to baking sheet. Stir-fry sweet potatoes in batches until tender and browned; remove to baking sheet. Add leeks; stir-fry 1 minute and remove to baking sheet.

5 Stir soy sauce mixture; add to skillet. Cook and stir until sugar dissolves. Add noodles; toss to coat. Gently stir in tofu, vegetables, peanuts, mint and cilantro; cook until heated through.

Makes 4 servings

fried tofu with sesame dipping sauce

3 tablespoons soy sauce or tamari

2 tablespoons unseasoned rice vinegar

2 teaspoons sugar

1 teaspoon sesame seeds, toasted*

1 teaspoon dark sesame oil

⅛ teaspoon red pepper flakes

1 package (14 ounces) extra firm tofu

2 tablespoons all-purpose flour

¼ cup rice milk or plain soymilk

1 tablespoon cornstarch

¾ cup panko bread crumbs

4 tablespoons vegetable oil

To toast sesame seeds, cook in small skillet over medium heat about 3 minutes or until seeds begin to pop and turn golden brown, stirring frequently.

1 For dipping sauce, whisk soy sauce, vinegar, sugar, sesame seeds, sesame oil and red pepper flakes in small bowl until well blended. Set aside.

2 Drain tofu and press between paper towels to remove excess water. Cut crosswise into four slices; cut each slice diagonally into triangles. Place flour in shallow dish. Stir rice milk into cornstarch in shallow bowl until smooth. Place panko in another shallow bowl.

3 Dip each piece of tofu in flour to lightly coat all sides; dip in rice milk mixture, turning to coat. Drain and roll in panko to coat.

4 Heat 2 tablespoons vegetable oil in large nonstick skillet over high heat. Reduce heat to medium; add half of tofu in single layer. Cook 1 to 2 minutes per side or until golden brown. Repeat with remaining tofu. Serve with dipping sauce.

Makes 4 servings

thai seitan stir-fry

1 package (8 ounces) seitan, drained and thinly sliced

1 jalapeño pepper,* halved and seeded

3 cloves garlic

1 piece peeled fresh ginger (about 1 inch)

⅓ cup soy sauce

¼ cup packed brown sugar

¼ cup lime juice (2 limes)

½ teaspoon red pepper flakes

¼ teaspoon salt

3 tablespoons vegetable oil

1 medium onion, chopped (about 2 cups)

2 red bell peppers, quartered and thinly sliced (about 2 cups)

2 cups broccoli florets

¼ cup shredded fresh basil

3 green onions, diagonally sliced

4 cups lightly packed baby spinach

3 cups hot cooked rice

¼ cup salted peanuts, chopped

Jalapeño peppers can sting and irritate the skin so wear rubber gloves when handling and do not touch your eyes.

1 Place seitan in medium bowl. Combine jalapeño, garlic and ginger in food processor; process until finely chopped. Add soy sauce, brown sugar, lime juice, red pepper flakes and salt; process until blended. Pour mixture over seitan; toss to coat. Marinate at least 20 minutes at room temperature.

2 Heat oil in wok or large skillet over high heat. Add onion, bell peppers and broccol; stir-fry 3 to 5 minutes. Add seitan, marinade and green onions; bring to a boil. Cook and stir 3 minutes or until vegetables are crisp-tender and seitan is heated through. Add half of spinach; stir-fry until beginning to wilt. Add remaining spinach; cook just until wilted.

3 Stir in basil just before serving. Serve over rice; sprinkle with peanuts.

Makes 4 to 6 servings

tip

Seitan is a meat substitute made from wheat that has had the starch washed away until only the wheat protein (gluten) remains. It is high in protein and has a meaty, chewy texture. Like tofu and tempeh, it will take on the flavor of whatever you marinate or cook with it.

tofu satay with peanut sauce

Satay

- **1 package (14 ounces) firm tofu, drained and pressed***
- **⅓ cup water**
- **⅓ cup soy sauce**
- **1 tablespoon sesame oil**
- **1 teaspoon minced garlic**
- **1 teaspoon minced fresh ginger**
- **24 white button mushrooms, trimmed**
- **1 large red bell pepper, cut into 12 pieces**

Peanut Sauce

- **1 can (14 ounces) unsweetened coconut milk**
- **½ cup creamy peanut butter**
- **2 tablespoons packed brown sugar**
- **1 tablespoon rice vinegar**
- **1 to 2 teaspoons red Thai curry paste**

*Place tofu between layers of paper towels. Place a weighted cutting board on top; let stand 15 to 30 minutes.

1 Cut tofu into 24 cubes. Combine water, soy sauce, sesame oil, garlic and ginger in small bowl. Place tofu, mushrooms and bell pepper in large resealable food storage bag. Add soy sauce mixture; seal bag and turn gently to coat. Marinate 30 minutes, turning occasionally. Soak eight 8-inch bamboo skewers in water 20 minutes.

2 Preheat oven to 400°F. Spray 13×9-inch glass baking dish with nonstick cooking spray.

3 Drain tofu mixture; discard marinade. Thread tofu, mushrooms and bell pepper alternately onto skewers. Place skewers in prepared baking dish.

4 Bake 25 minutes or until tofu cubes are lightly browned and vegetables are softened.

5 Meanwhile, whisk coconut milk, peanut butter, brown sugar, vinegar and curry paste in small saucepan over medium heat. Bring to a boil, stirring constantly. Immediately reduce heat to low; cook over very low heat about 20 minutes or until thick and creamy, stirring frequently. Serve satay with sauce.

Makes 4 servings

ma po tofu

1 package (14 ounces) firm tofu, drained and pressed*

2 tablespoons soy sauce

2 teaspoons minced fresh ginger

1 cup vegetable broth, divided

2 tablespoons black bean sauce

1 tablespoon Thai sweet chili sauce

1 tablespoon cornstarch

2 tablespoons vegetable oil

1 green bell pepper, cut into bite-size pieces

2 cloves garlic, minced

1½ cups broccoli florets

¼ cup chopped fresh cilantro (optional)

Hot cooked rice

*Cut tofu in half horizontally and place it between layers of paper towels. Place a weighted cutting board on top; let stand 15 to 30 minutes.

1 Cut tofu into cubes. Place in shallow dish; sprinkle with soy sauce and ginger.

2 Whisk ¼ cup broth, black bean sauce, chili sauce and cornstarch in small bowl until smooth and well blended; set aside.

3 Heat oil in wok or large skillet over high heat. Add bell pepper and garlic; stir-fry 2 minutes. Add remaining ¾ cup broth and broccoli; bring to a boil. Reduce heat; cover and simmer 3 minutes or until broccoli is crisp-tender.

4 Stir sauce mixture; add to wok. Cook and stir 1 minute or until sauce boils and thickens. Stir in tofu; simmer, uncovered, until heated through. Sprinkle with cilantro, if desired. Serve with rice.

Makes 4 servings

tip

Regular or brick tofu (sometimes called Chinese tofu) is found in the refrigerated section of the supermarket in the produce section or near the dairy case; it comes sealed in a plastic tub filled with water. There is usually a choice of soft, medium, firm or extra firm. Once opened, tofu will keep in the refrigerator up to 4 days. The water should be drained and replaced daily.

teriyaki tempeh with pineapple

1 package (8 ounces)
    unseasoned tempeh,
    cut in half crosswise

1 to 1½ cups pineapple
    teriyaki sauce

1 cup uncooked rice

½ cup matchstick-size carrots

½ cup snow peas

½ cup matchstick-size red bell
    pepper strips

4 fresh pineapple rings

1 Place 1 cup water and tempeh in large deep skillet; bring to a boil over high heat. Reduce heat to low; simmer 10 minutes. Drain water; add 1 cup teriyaki sauce to tempeh in skillet. Bring to a simmer over medium heat; simmer 10 minutes, turning tempeh occasionally. Drain and reserve teriyaki sauce; add additional sauce, if necessary, to make ½ cup.

2 Meanwhile, cook rice according to package directions. Heat reserved teriyaki sauce in wok or large nonstick skillet over medium-high heat. Add carrots, snow peas and bell pepper; cook and stir 4 to 6 minutes or until crisp-tender. Add rice; stir to combine. Add additional teriyaki sauce, if desired.

3 Prepare grill for direct cooking. Grill tempeh and pineapple rings over medium-high heat 10 minutes, turning once. Cut tempeh in half; serve with rice and pineapple.

Makes 4 servings

ISLAND TEMPEH SANDWICHES: Omit rice and vegetables. Serve tempeh and pineapple on soft rolls with arugula, additional teriyaki sauce and vegan mayonnaise.

buddha's delight

1 package (1 ounce) dried black Chinese mushrooms

1 package (14 ounces) firm tofu, drained

1 tablespoon peanut or vegetable oil

2 cups diagonally cut 1-inch asparagus pieces

1 medium onion, cut into thin wedges

2 cloves garlic, minced

½ cup vegetable broth

3 tablespoons hoisin sauce

¼ cup coarsely chopped fresh cilantro or thinly sliced green onions

1 Place mushrooms in medium bowl; cover with warm water. Soak 20 to 40 minutes or until soft. Drain mushrooms; strain and reserve soaking liquid. Cut off and discard stems; cut caps into thin slices.

2 Meanwhile, place tofu on plate or cutting board lined with paper towels; cover with additional paper towels and place flat, heavy object on top. Let stand 15 minutes. Cut tofu into ¾-inch cubes or triangles.

3 Heat oil in wok or large skillet over medium-high heat. Add asparagus, onion and garlic; stir-fry 4 minutes.

4 Add mushrooms, ¼ cup reserved mushroom liquid, broth and hoisin sauce; cook over medium-low heat 2 to 3 minutes or until asparagus is crisp-tender, .

5 Stir in tofu; heat through. Ladle into shallow bowls; sprinkle with cilantro.

Makes 2 servings

dragon tofu

1 package (14 ounces) firm tofu, drained

¼ cup soy sauce

1 tablespoon creamy peanut butter

1 medium zucchini

1 medium yellow squash

1 medium red bell pepper

2 teaspoons peanut or vegetable oil

½ teaspoon hot chili oil

2 cloves garlic, minced

2 cups packed torn spinach leaves

¼ cup coarsely chopped cashews or peanuts

1 Press tofu between paper towels; cut into ¾-inch squares or triangles. Place in single layer in shallow dish. Whisk soy sauce into peanut butter in small bowl. Pour mixture over tofu; stir gently to coat all sides. Let stand 20 minutes.

2 Meanwhile, cut zucchini and yellow squash lengthwise into ¼-inch-thick slices; cut each slice into 2-inch strips. Cut bell pepper into 2-inch strips.

3 Heat peanut oil and chili oil in large skillet over medium-high heat. Add garlic, zucchini, yellow squash and bell pepper; stir-fry 3 minutes. Add tofu mixture; cook 2 minutes or until tofu is heated through and sauce is slightly thickened, stirring occasionally. Stir in spinach; remove from heat. Sprinkle with cashews before serving.

Makes 2 servings

tofu, vegetable and curry stir-fry

1 package (14 ounces) extra firm tofu, drained

¾ cup coconut milk

2 tablespoons fresh lime juice

1 tablespoon curry powder

2 teaspoons dark sesame oil, divided

4 cups broccoli florets (1½-inch pieces)

2 medium red bell peppers, cut into short, thin strips

1 medium red onion, cut into thin wedges

¼ teaspoon salt

Hot cooked brown rice (optional)

1 Press tofu between paper towels; cut into ¾-inch cubes. Combine coconut milk, lime juice and curry powder in medium bowl.

2 Heat 1 teaspoon oil in large nonstick skillet over medium heat. Add tofu; cook 10 minutes or until lightly browned on all sides, turning cubes often. Remove to plate.

3 Add remaining 1 teaspoon oil to skillet. Add broccoli, bell peppers and onion; stir-fry over high heat about 5 minutes or until vegetables are crisp-tender.

4 Add tofu and coconut milk mixture; cook and stir until mixture comes to a boil. Stir in salt. Serve immediately with rice, if desired.

Makes 4 servings

BEANS & GRAINS

barley and swiss chard skillet casserole

1 cup water

1 cup chopped red bell pepper

1 cup chopped green bell pepper

¾ cup uncooked quick-cooking barley

⅛ teaspoon garlic powder

⅛ teaspoon red pepper flakes

2 cups packed coarsely chopped Swiss chard*

1 cup canned navy beans, rinsed and drained

1 cup quartered cherry tomatoes

¼ cup chopped fresh basil

1 tablespoon olive oil

2 tablespoons Italian-seasoned dry bread crumbs

Fresh spinach or beet greens can be substituted for Swiss chard.

1 Preheat broiler.

2 Bring water to a boil in large ovenproof skillet. Add bell peppers, barley, garlic powder and red pepper flakes; cover and simmer over low heat 10 minutes or until liquid is absorbed. Remove from heat.

3 Stir in chard, beans, tomatoes, basil and oil. Sprinkle with bread crumbs. Broil 2 minutes or until golden.

Makes 4 servings

quinoa and mango salad

1 cup uncooked quinoa

2 cups water

2 cups cubed peeled mangoes (about 2 large)

½ cup sliced green onions

½ cup dried cranberries

2 tablespoons chopped fresh parsley

¼ cup extra virgin olive oil

1½ tablespoons white wine vinegar

1 teaspoon Dijon mustard

½ teaspoon salt

⅛ teaspoon black pepper

1 Place quinoa in fine-mesh strainer; rinse well under cold running water. Combine quinoa and 2 cups water in medium saucepan; bring to a boil over high heat. Reduce heat to low; cover and simmer 10 to 12 minutes or until quinoa is tender and water is absorbed. Stir quinoa; cover and let stand 15 minutes. Transfer to large bowl; cover and refrigerate at least 1 hour.

2 Add mangoes, green onions, cranberries and parsley to quinoa; mix well.

3 Whisk oil, vinegar, mustard, salt and pepper in small bowl until blended. Pour over quinoa mixture; mix well.

Makes 8 servings

TIP: This salad can be made several hours ahead and refrigerated. Let stand at room temperature at least 30 minutes before serving.

NOTE: Quinoa may seem new to many Americans but it is actually an ancient grain that was grown by the Incas. This tiny round whole grain is higher in protein than other grains and contains all eight essential amino acids, so it is considered a complete protein.

jambalaya-style rice and beans

2 cups chopped green bell peppers

1 can (about 15 ounces) dark red kidney beans, rinsed and drained

1 can (about 14 ounces) diced tomatoes with green bell peppers and onions

1 cup chopped onion

1 cup sliced celery

1 cup water, divided

¾ cup uncooked long grain white rice

1¼ teaspoons salt

1 teaspoon hot pepper sauce

½ teaspoon dried thyme

½ teaspoon red pepper flakes

3 bay leaves

1 package (8 ounces) seitan, chopped

2 tablespoons extra virgin olive oil

½ cup chopped fresh parsley

Additional hot pepper sauce (optional)

Slow Cooker Directions

1 Combine bell peppers, beans, tomatoes, onion, celery, ½ cup water, rice, salt, hot pepper sauce, thyme, red pepper flakes and bay leaves in slow cooker. Cover; cook on LOW 4 to 5 hours. Remove and discard bay leaves.

2 Heat oil in large nonstick skillet over medium-high heat. Add seitan; cook 2 minutes or until lightly browned, stirring occasionally.

3 Add seitan to slow cooker. Add remaining ½ cup water to skillet; bring to a boil over high heat. Boil 1 minute, scraping up browned bits from bottom of skillet. Add liquid and parsley to slow cooker; stir gently to blend. Serve with additional hot pepper sauce, if desired.

Makes 6 to 8 servings

four-pepper black bean fajitas

1 can (about 15 ounces) black beans, rinsed and drained

¼ cup water

3 tablespoons olive oil, divided

2 tablespoons lime juice

1 canned chipotle pepper in adobo sauce

1 clove garlic, minced

¼ teaspoon salt

1 medium red bell pepper, cut into strips

1 medium green bell pepper, cut into strips

1 medium yellow bell pepper, cut into strips

2 medium onions, cut into ¼-inch wedges

8 (8-inch) flour tortillas

¼ cup chopped fresh cilantro

Lime wedges (optional)

1 Combine beans, water, 2 tablespoons oil, lime juice, chipotle, garlic and salt in food processor or blender; process until smooth. Place in medium microwavable bowl. Cover with plastic wrap; set aside.

2 Heat remaining 1 tablespoon oil in large skillet over medium-high heat. Add bell peppers and onions; cook and stir 12 minutes or until vegetables begin to brown.

3 Microwave bean mixture on HIGH 2 to 3 minutes or until heated through. Heat tortillas according to package directions.

4 Divide bean mixture among tortillas; top with bell pepper mixture. Sprinkle with cilantro; serve with lime wedges, if desired.

Makes 4 servings

lentil rice curry

2 tablespoons olive oil

1 cup sliced green onions

2 tablespoons minced fresh ginger

3 cloves garlic, minced

2 teaspoons curry powder

½ teaspoon ground cumin

½ teaspoon ground turmeric

3 cups water

1 can (about 14 ounces) stewed tomatoes, undrained

½ teaspoon salt

1 cup uncooked red lentils, rinsed and sorted

1 large head cauliflower (about 1¼ pounds), broken into florets

1 tablespoon lemon juice

Fragrant Basmati Rice (recipe follows) *or* 4 cups hot cooked jasmine rice

1 Heat oil in large saucepan over medium heat. Add green onions, ginger, garlic, curry powder, cumin and turmeric; cook and stir 5 minutes. Add water, tomatoes and salt; bring to a boil over high heat.

2 Stir in lentils. Reduce heat to low; cover and simmer 35 to 40 minutes or until lentils are tender. Add cauliflower and lemon juice; cover and simmer 8 to 10 minutes or until cauliflower is tender.

3 Meanwhile prepare Fragrant Basmati Rice. Serve with lentil curry.

Makes 6 servings

fragrant basmati rice

2 cups apple juice

¾ cup water

½ teaspoon salt

1½ cups white basmati or Texmati rice

2 thin slices fresh ginger

1 piece cinnamon stick (2 inches long)

Bring apple juice, water and salt to a boil in medium saucepan. Add rice, ginger and cinnamon stick; cover and simmer over low heat 25 to 30 minutes or until liquid is absorbed. Remove and discard ginger and cinnamon stick.

Makes 4 cups

quinoa and roasted corn

1 cup uncooked quinoa

2 cups water

½ teaspoon salt

4 ears corn *or* **2 cups frozen corn**

¼ cup plus 1 tablespoon vegetable oil, divided

1 cup chopped green onions, divided

1 teaspoon coarse salt

1 cup quartered grape tomatoes or chopped plum tomatoes, drained*

1 cup canned black beans, rinsed and drained

2 tablespoons lime juice

¼ teaspoon grated lime peel

¼ teaspoon sugar

¼ teaspoon ground cumin

¼ teaspoon black pepper

*Place tomatoes in fine-mesh strainer and place in sink or over bowl 10 to 15 minutes.

1 Place quinoa in fine-mesh strainer; rinse well under cold running water. Combine quinoa, 2 cups water and ½ teaspoon salt in medium saucepan; bring to a boil over high heat. Reduce heat to low; cover and simmer 15 to 18 minutes or until quinoa is tender and water is absorbed. Transfer to large bowl.

2 Meanwhile, remove husks and silk from corn; cut kernels off cobs. Heat ¼ cup oil in large skillet over medium-high heat. Add corn; cook 10 to 12 minutes or until tender and lightly browned, stirring occasionally. Stir in ⅔ cup green onions and coarse salt; cook and stir 2 minutes. Add corn mixture to quinoa. Gently stir in tomatoes and black beans.

3 Combine lime juice, lime peel, sugar, cumin and black pepper in small bowl. Whisk in remaining 1 tablespoon oil until blended. Pour over quinoa mixture; toss lightly to coat. Sprinkle with remaining ⅓ cup green onions. Serve warm or chilled.

Makes 6 to 8 servings

picante pintos and rice

2 cups dried pinto beans, rinsed and sorted

1 can (about 14 ounces) stewed tomatoes

1 cup coarsely chopped onion

¾ cup coarsely chopped green bell pepper

¼ cup sliced celery

4 cloves garlic, minced

½ small jalapeño pepper,* seeded and chopped

2 teaspoons dried oregano

2 teaspoons chili powder

½ teaspoon ground red pepper

2 cups chopped kale

3 cups hot cooked brown rice

*Jalapeño peppers can sting and irritate the skin, so wear rubber gloves when handling peppers and do not touch your eyes.

1 Place beans in large saucepan; add water to cover by 2 inches. Bring to a boil over high heat; boil 2 minutes. Remove from heat; cover and let stand 1 hour. Drain beans; discard water. Return beans to saucepan.

2 Add 2 cups water, tomatoes, onion, bell pepper, celery, garlic, jalapeño, oregano, chili powder and ground red pepper to saucepan; bring to a boil over high heat. Reduce heat to low; cover and simmer about 1½ hours or until beans are tender, stirring occasionally.

3 Gently stir kale into bean mixture. Simmer, uncovered, 30 minutes. Serve over rice.

Makes 8 servings

tip

Dried beans are a great alternative to canned beans—they are cheaper and have a firmer texture and fresher flavor. Look for dried beans in plastic packages or in bulk; they will keep up to a year in your pantry. To save time and prepare for future meals, cook more dried beans than you need and freeze the extras in containers or small resealable food storage bags.

bulgur with asparagus and spring herbs

⅔ cup uncooked bulgur

2 cups sliced asparagus (1-inch pieces)

½ cup frozen peas, thawed

⅔ cup chopped fresh Italian parsley

2 teaspoons finely chopped fresh mint

3 tablespoons lemon juice

1 tablespoon orange juice

1 tablespoon extra virgin olive oil

⅛ teaspoon salt

⅛ teaspoon black pepper

1 Prepare bulgur according to package directions; drain well.

2 Steam asparagus in steamer basket over boiling water 3 to 4 minutes or until bright green and crisp-tender. Cool under cold running water; drain well and blot dry with paper towels.

3 Combine bulgur, asparagus, peas, parsley and mint in large bowl. Whisk lemon juice, orange juice, oil, salt and pepper in small bowl. Pour over bulgur mixture; toss gently.

Makes 4 servings

NOTE: Bulgur is a whole grain that's high in fiber and protein. It's also a good source of iron, magnesium and B vitamins.

spanish rice with chorizo

1 tablespoon olive oil

12 ounces soy chorizo, casings removed, sliced

1 green bell pepper, diced

1½ cups uncooked instant rice

1 can (about 14 ounces) diced tomatoes

1 cup vegetable broth or water

2 green onions, chopped

Salt and black pepper

1 Heat oil in large nonstick skillet over medium heat. Add soy chorizo and bell pepper; cook and stir 5 minutes or until bell pepper is tender. Stir in rice, tomatoes, broth and green onions; bring to a boil over high heat.

2 Reduce heat to medium-low; cover and simmer 8 to 10 minutes or until liquid is absorbed and rice is tender. Season with salt and black pepper.

Makes 4 servings

french lentil salad

1½ cups dried lentils, rinsed and sorted

¼ cup chopped walnuts

4 green onions, finely chopped

3 tablespoons balsamic vinegar

2 tablespoons chopped fresh parsley

1 tablespoon olive oil

¾ teaspoon salt

½ teaspoon dried thyme

¼ teaspoon black pepper

Lettuce leaves (optional)

1 Combine 2 quarts water and lentils in large saucepan; bring to a boil over high heat. Reduce heat to low; cover and simmer 30 minutes or until lentils are tender, stirring occasionally. Drain lentils.

2 Meanwhile, preheat oven to 375°F. Spread walnuts in single layer on baking sheet. Bake 5 minutes or until lightly browned. Cool completely on baking sheet.

3 Combine lentils, green onions, vinegar, parsley, oil, salt, thyme and pepper in large bowl; mix well. Cover and refrigerate 1 hour or until cool.

4 Serve on lettuce leaves, if desired. Top with toasted walnuts before serving.

Makes 4 servings

tip

Lentils come in a variety of colors, with greenish-brown being the most commonly available. For a change of pace, try French green lentils or black beluga lentils if you can find them. (Indian markets always have a huge variety of lentils, which are referred to as "dal.") Always purchase lentils from a market with high turnover to ensure the ones you get are reasonably fresh. While they do have a long shelf life, lentils are best used within a year.

VEGETABLE HEAVEN

roasted vegetable salad with capers and walnuts

1 pound small brussels sprouts, trimmed

1 pound unpeeled small Yukon Gold potatoes, cut into halves

¼ teaspoon salt

¼ teaspoon black pepper

¼ teaspoon dried rosemary

5 tablespoons olive oil, divided

1 red bell pepper, cut into bite-size pieces

¼ cup walnuts, coarsely chopped

2 tablespoons capers, drained

1½ tablespoons white wine vinegar

1 Preheat oven to 400°F.

2 Slash bottoms of brussels sprouts; place in shallow roasting pan. Add potatoes; sprinkle with salt, black pepper and rosemary. Drizzle with 3 tablespoons oil; toss to coat.

3 Roast 20 minutes. Stir in bell pepper; roast 15 minutes or until tender. Transfer to large bowl; stir in walnuts and capers.

4 Whisk remaining 2 tablespoons oil and vinegar in small bowl until blended. Pour over salad; toss to coat. Serve at room temperature.

Makes 6 to 8 servings

mushroom gratin

4 tablespoons dairy-free margarine, divided

1 small onion, minced

8 ounces (about 2½ cups) sliced cremini mushrooms

2 cloves garlic, minced

4 cups cooked elbow macaroni, rotini or penne pasta

2 tablespoons all-purpose flour

1 cup unsweetened soymilk

½ teaspoon salt

½ teaspoon black pepper

½ teaspoon dry mustard

½ cup fresh bread crumbs

1 tablespoon extra virgin olive oil

1 Preheat oven to 350°F. Spray shallow baking dish or casserole with nonstick cooking spray. Melt 2 tablespoons margarine in large skillet over medium-high heat. Add onion; cook and stir 2 minutes. Add mushrooms and garlic; cook and stir 6 to 8 minutes or until vegetables soften. Remove from heat. Stir in macaroni.

2 Melt remaining 2 tablespoons margarine in medium saucepan over low heat. Whisk in flour; cook and stir 2 minutes without browning. Stir in soymilk. Bring to a boil over medium-high heat, whisking constantly. Reduce heat to maintain a simmer. Add salt, pepper and mustard; whisk 5 to 7 minutes or until sauce thickens.

3 Pour sauce over mushroom mixture in skillet; stir to coat. Spoon into prepared baking dish. Top with bread crumbs; drizzle with oil.

4 Cover and bake 15 minutes. Uncover and bake 10 minutes or until bubbly and browned.

Makes 8 servings

brussels sprouts in orange sauce

4 cups fresh brussels sprouts

1 cup fresh orange juice

½ cup water

1 teaspoon grated orange peel

½ teaspoon cornstarch

¼ teaspoon red pepper flakes (optional)

¼ teaspoon ground cinnamon

Salt and black pepper

1 Combine brussels sprouts, orange juice, water, orange peel, cornstarch, red pepper flakes, if desired, and cinnamon in medium saucepan. Cover and simmer 6 to 7 minutes or until sprouts are nearly tender.

2 Uncover and simmer until most of liquid has evaporated, stirring occasionally. Season with salt and pepper.

Makes 4 servings

apple stuffed acorn squash

¼ cup raisins

2 acorn squash (about 4 inches in diameter)

2½ tablespoons dairy-free margarine, melted, divided

2 tablespoons sugar

¼ teaspoon ground cinnamon

2 medium Fuji apples, cut into ½-inch pieces

1 Place raisins in small bowl; cover with warm water. Soak 20 minutes. Preheat oven to 375°F.

2 Cut squash into quarters; remove seeds. Place squash on baking sheet; brush with ½ tablespoon margarine. Combine sugar and cinnamon in small bowl; sprinkle half of cinnamon mixture over squash. Bake 10 minutes.

3 Meanwhile, drain raisins. Melt remaining 2 tablespoons margarine in medium saucepan over medium heat. Add apples, raisins and remaining cinnamon mixture; cook and stir 2 minutes. Top partially baked squash evenly with apple mixture. Bake 30 to 35 minutes or until apples and squash are tender. Serve warm.

Makes 8 servings

grilled spaghetti squash with black beans and zucchini

1 spaghetti squash (about 2 pounds)

2 medium zucchini, cut lengthwise into ¼-inch-thick slices

3 tablespoons olive oil, divided

2 cups chopped seeded fresh tomatoes

1 can (about 15 ounces) black beans, rinsed and drained

2 tablespoons chopped fresh basil

2 tablespoons red wine vinegar

1 clove garlic, minced

½ teaspoon salt

1 Prepare grill for direct cooking. Pierce spaghetti squash in several places with fork. Place in center of large piece of heavy-duty foil. Bring two long sides of foil together above squash; fold down in series of locked folds, allowing room for heat circulation and expansion. Fold short ends up and over again. Press folds firmly to seal foil packet.

2 Grill squash, covered, over medium heat 45 minutes to 1 hour or until easily depressed with back of long-handled spoon, turning one quarter turn every 15 minutes. Remove squash from grill; let stand in foil 10 to 15 minutes.

3 Meanwhile, brush both sides of zucchini slices with 1 tablespoon oil. Grill, uncovered, 4 minutes or until tender, turning once. Cut into bite-size pieces.

4 Remove spaghetti squash from foil; cut in half and remove seeds. Separate squash into strands with two forks; place on serving plate.

5 Combine zucchini, tomatoes, beans and basil in medium bowl. Whisk remaining 2 tablespoons oil, vinegar, garlic and salt in small bowl until well blended. Add to vegetables; toss gently to coat. Serve vegetable mixture over squash.

Makes 4 servings

vegetable sushi maki

6 sheets toasted sushi nori

1 teaspoon wasabi or prepared mustard

1½ cups cooked Sushi Rice (recipe follows)

1 ripe avocado, thinly sliced

4 thin strips peeled cucumber

1 cup spinach leaves, thinly sliced

½ cup thinly sliced carrot, steamed

4 teaspoons toasted sesame seeds

Pickled ginger

Soy sauce

1 Place one sheet of nori on flat work surface. Cover bottom third of sheet with thin layer of wasabi. Spread about ⅓ cup rice on top of wasabi, leaving 1-inch border along bottom edge. Layer avocado, cucumber, spinach, carrot and sesame seeds on top of rice.

2 Moisten top edge of nori sheet. Lift bottom edge and press into rice; roll up and press gently to seal. Repeat with remaining ingredients.

3 Cut rolls crosswise into 1-inch slices with sharp knife, wiping knife with warm water if it gets sticky. Serve with pickled ginger and soy sauce.

Makes 6 rolls

sushi rice

1¾ cups water

½ teaspoon salt

1 cup sushi rice or short grain brown rice

⅓ cup rice vinegar

1 tablespoon sugar

1 teaspoon salt

1 Bring water and salt to a boil in small saucepan. Add rice; stir. Reduce heat to low; cover and simmer 20 minutes for sushi rice or 40 minutes for brown rice.

2 Remove rice from heat; let stand 5 minutes. Remove rice from saucepan; let cool slightly. While still warm, gently stir vinegar, sugar and salt into rice.

Makes 2 cups

greek salad with dairy-free "feta"

Dairy-Free "Feta"

1 package (14 ounces) firm or extra firm tofu

½ cup extra virgin olive oil

¼ cup lemon juice

2 teaspoons salt

2 teaspoons Greek or Italian seasoning

½ teaspoon black pepper

1 teaspoon onion powder

½ teaspoon garlic powder

Salad

1 pint grape tomatoes, halved

2 seedless cucumbers, quartered lengthwise and sliced

1 yellow bell pepper, slivered

1 small red onion, cut in thin slices

1 For "feta," cut tofu crosswise into two pieces, each about 1 inch thick. Place on cutting board lined with paper towels; top with layer of paper towels. Place weighted baking dish on top of tofu. Let stand 30 minutes to drain. Pat tofu dry; crumble into large bowl.

2 Combine oil, lemon juice, salt, Greek seasoning and black pepper in small jar with lid; shake until well blended. Reserve ¼ cup mixture for salad dressing.

3 Add onion powder and garlic powder to remaining oil mixture; pour over tofu and toss gently. Cover and refrigerate 2 hours or overnight.

4 For salad, combine tomatoes, cucumbers, bell pepper and onion in serving bowl. Add tofu and reserved dressing; toss gently.

Makes 4 to 6 servings

parsnip patties

1 pound parsnips, peeled and cut into ¾-inch chunks

4 tablespoons dairy-free margarine, divided

¼ cup chopped onion

¼ cup all-purpose flour

⅓ cup dairy-free milk

2 teaspoons chopped fresh chives

Salt and black pepper

¾ cup fresh bread crumbs

2 tablespoons vegetable oil

1 Fill medium saucepan with 1 inch of water; bring to a boil over high heat. Add parsnips; cover and cook over medium heat 10 minutes or until fork-tender. Drain. Place in large bowl; coarsely mash with fork.

2 Melt 2 tablespoons margarine in same saucepan over medium-high heat. Add onion; cook and stir until translucent. Whisk in flour until bubbly and lightly browned. Whisk in dairy-free milk; cook and stir until thickened. Stir into mashed parsnips. Stir in chives; season with salt and pepper.

3 Shape parsnip mixture into four patties. Spread bread crumbs on plate. Dip patties in bread crumbs to coat all sides. Place on waxed paper-lined plate; refrigerate 2 hours.

4 Heat remaining 2 tablespoons margarine and oil in large skillet over medium-high heat until margarine is melted and bubbly. Add patties; cook 5 minutes per side or until browned.

Makes 4 servings

rich roasted sesame vegetables

1 carrot, quartered lengthwise and cut into 2-inch pieces

1 sweet potato, peeled and cut into ¾-inch cubes

½ red bell pepper, cut into 1-inch cubes

½ medium onion, cut into ½-inch wedges

1 tablespoon dark sesame oil, divided

2 teaspoons sugar, divided

¼ teaspoon salt

1 Preheat oven to 425°F. Line large baking sheet with foil.

2 Place carrot, sweet potato, bell pepper and onion on baking sheet. Sprinkle with 2 teaspoons oil, 1 teaspoon sugar and salt; toss gently to coat. Arrange vegetables in single layer.

3 Roast 20 minutes or until edges are browned and sweet potatoes are tender when pierced with fork, stirring once halfway through cooking time. Sprinkle with remaining 1 teaspoon oil and 1 teaspoon sugar; toss gently to coat.

Makes 2 servings

TIP: Before serving, sprinkle vegetables with rice vinegar or lime juice.

garlicky mustard greens

2 pounds mustard greens

1 tablespoon olive oil

1 cup chopped onion

2 cloves garlic, minced

¾ cup chopped red bell pepper

½ cup vegetable broth

1 tablespoon cider vinegar

1 teaspoon sugar

1 Remove stems and any wilted leaves from greens. Stack several leaves; roll up and cut crosswise into 1-inch slices. Repeat with remaining greens.

2 Heat oil in large saucepan over medium heat. Add onion and garlic; cook and stir 5 minutes or until onion is tender. Stir in greens, bell pepper and broth; cover and cook over low heat 25 minutes or until greens are tender, stirring occasionally.

3 Combine vinegar and sugar in small bowl; stir until sugar is dissolved. Stir into cooked greens; remove from heat. Serve immediately.

Makes 4 servings

coconut butternut squash

1 tablespoon dairy-free
   margarine

½ cup chopped onion

1 pound butternut squash,
   peeled, seeded and cut
   into 1-inch pieces

1 pound sweet potatoes,
   peeled and cut into
   1-inch pieces

1 can (about 14 ounces)
   coconut milk*

3 tablespoons packed
   brown sugar, divided

½ teaspoon salt

½ teaspoon ground cinnamon

¼ teaspoon ground nutmeg

¼ teaspoon ground allspice

1 tablespoon grated fresh
   ginger

*Shake vigorously before opening to mix
thoroughly.

1 Melt margarine in large skillet over medium-high heat. Add onion; cook and stir 4 minutes or until translucent. Add squash, sweet potatoes, coconut milk, 1 tablespoon brown sugar, salt, cinnamon, nutmeg and allspice; bring to a boil over medium-high heat.

2 Reduce heat to low; cover and simmer 10 minutes. Uncover and cook 5 minutes or until vegetables are tender, stirring frequently. Remove from heat. Stir in ginger.

3 Transfer mixture to blender or food processor; blend until smooth. Spoon into serving bowls; sprinkle with remaining 2 tablespoons brown sugar.

Makes 6 servings

tip

When selecting a butternut or other winter squash, choose one that is rock solid. Press hard to make sure there are no soft spots, as these would indicate the squash is immature or way past its prime. Make sure the stem is in place and firm—if the stem is missing, bacteria can enter and spoil the flesh. Butternut squash will keep for months if it's in good shape to begin with and stored in a dry place at cool room temperature.

DECADENT DESSERTS

maui waui cookies

2 cups all-purpose flour

1 cup quick oats

½ teaspoon baking powder

½ teaspoon salt

½ teaspoon ground cinnamon

¼ teaspoon baking soda

1 cup sugar

1 cup (2 sticks) dairy-free margarine, softened

Prepared egg replacer equal to 1 egg

¾ cup coarsely chopped salted macadamia nuts

½ cup flaked coconut

Pineapple Glaze (optional, recipe follows)

1 Preheat oven to 375°F. Line cookie sheets with parchment paper. Combine flour, oats, baking powder, salt, cinnamon and baking soda in small bowl.

2 Beat margarine and sugar in large bowl with electric mixer at medium-high speed until creamy. Beat in egg replacer. Beat in flour mixture, ½ cup at a time, until well blended. Stir in macadamia nuts and coconut. Drop dough by 2 tablespoonfuls about 1 ½ inches apart onto prepared cookie sheets.

3 Bake 16 minutes or until cookies are set and edges are golden brown. Cool on cookie sheets 2 minutes; remove parchment paper to wire racks to cool completely.

4 Prepare Pineapple Glaze, if desired; drizzle over cookies.

Makes about 3 dozen cookies

PINEAPPLE GLAZE: Place 1 ½ tablespoons melted dairy-free margarine in medium bowl. Stir in 1 cup powdered sugar until blended. Gradually add 4 to 6 teaspoons unsweetened pineapple juice until glaze reaches consistency for drizzling.

intense chocolate ice cream

2 cups plain rice milk, divided

¼ cup tapioca flour

¼ cup unsweetened cocoa powder

6 tablespoons sugar

¼ teaspoon salt

⅓ cup dairy-free semisweet chocolate chips

½ teaspoon vanilla

Fresh berries (optional)

1 Whisk ½ cup rice milk, tapioca flour and cocoa in medium saucepan until smooth. Add remaining 1½ cups rice milk; mix well. Stir in sugar and salt until blended. Cook over medium heat, stirring constantly, until mixture thickens to consistency of pudding. Remove from heat; stir in chocolate chips and vanilla until mixture is melted and smooth.

2 Transfer to medium bowl; cover and refrigerate 2 hours or until cold.

3 Pour into ice cream maker; process according to manufacturer's directions. Serve with berries, if desired.

Makes 4 servings

mixed berry crisp

6 cups mixed berries, thawed if frozen

¾ cup packed brown sugar, divided

¼ cup quick-cooking tapioca

Juice of ½ lemon

1 teaspoon ground cinnamon

½ cup all-purpose flour

6 tablespoons cold dairy-free margarine, cut into small pieces

½ cup sliced almonds

1 Preheat oven to 375°F. Grease 8- or 9-inch square baking pan.

2 Combine berries, ¼ cup brown sugar, tapioca, lemon juice and cinnamon in large bowl. Pour into prepared pan.

3 Combine flour, remaining ½ cup brown sugar and margarine in food processor; pulse until mixture resembles coarse crumbs. Add almonds; pulse until combined. (Leave some large pieces of almonds.) Sprinkle over berry mixture.

4 Bake 20 to 30 minutes or until golden brown.

Makes about 9 servings

carrot ginger cupcakes

3 cups all-purpose flour

⅓ cup coarsely chopped pecans, plus additional for garnish

2 teaspoons baking powder

1 teaspoon baking soda

1 teaspoon salt

½ teaspoon ground cinnamon

¾ cup water

3 tablespoons ground flaxseed

1½ cups granulated sugar

½ cup vegetable oil

½ cup (1 stick) dairy-free margarine

1 tablespoon vanilla

1 pound carrots, shredded

Grated peel of 2 oranges

Juice of 1 orange

2 tablespoons grated fresh ginger

Frosting

½ cup (1 stick) dairy-free margarine

4½ cups powdered sugar

¼ cup orange juice

1 tablespoon grated fresh ginger

1 teaspoon vanilla

1 Preheat oven to 350°F. Line 24 standard (2½-inch) muffin cups with paper baking cups.

2 Whisk flour, ⅓ cup pecans, baking powder, baking soda, salt and cinnamon in medium bowl. Combine water and flaxseed in small saucepan; bring to a boil over medium-high heat. Reduce heat to low; simmer 3 minutes. Cool to room temperature.

3 Beat granulated sugar, oil and ½ cup margarine in large bowl with electric mixer at medium speed until light and fluffy. Beat in flaxseed mixture and 1 tablespoon vanilla. Add carrots, orange peel, juice of 1 orange and 2 tablespoons ginger; mix well. Add flour mixture; mix just until combined. Spoon batter evenly into prepared muffin cups.

4 Bake 22 to 25 minutes or until toothpick inserted into centers comes out clean. Cool in pans 10 minutes; remove to wire racks to cool completely.

5 For frosting, beat ½ cup margarine in large bowl with electric mixer at medium speed until creamy. Gradually add powdered sugar, beating well after each addition. Beat in ¼ cup orange juice, 1 tablespoon ginger and 1 teaspoon vanilla. Beat at medium-high speed 2 minutes or until well blended and fluffy.

6 Frost cupcakes; sprinkle with additional pecans. Refrigerate until ready to serve.

oat-apricot snack cake

1½ cups all-purpose flour

1 teaspoon baking soda

1 teaspoon ground cinnamon

½ teaspoon salt

1 container (6 ounces) plain soy yogurt

¾ cup packed brown sugar

½ cup granulated sugar

⅓ cup vegetable oil

¼ cup silken tofu, stirred until smooth

4 tablespoons orange juice, divided

2 teaspoons vanilla

2 cups old-fashioned oats

1 cup chopped dried apricots

1 cup powdered sugar

1 Preheat oven to 350°F. Spray 13×9-inch baking pan with nonstick cooking spray.

2 Combine flour, baking soda, cinnamon and salt in medium bowl. Whisk yogurt, brown sugar, granulated sugar, oil, tofu, 2 tablespoons orange juice and vanilla in large bowl. Add flour mixture; stir until blended. Stir in oats and apricots. Spread batter in prepared pan.

3 Bake 20 to 25 minutes or until toothpick inserted into center comes out clean. Cool completely in pan on wire rack.

4 Whisk powdered sugar and remaining 2 tablespoons orange juice in small bowl until smooth. Drizzle glaze over cake.

Makes 24 servings

choco-peanut butter popcorn

⅓ cup dairy-free semisweet chocolate chips

3 tablespoons natural creamy peanut butter

1 tablespoon dairy-free margarine

4 cups popped popcorn

½ cup powdered sugar

1 Microwave chocolate chips, peanut butter and margarine in medium microwavable bowl on HIGH 30 seconds; stir. Microwave 30 seconds or until melted and smooth. Pour mixture over popcorn in large bowl, stirring until evenly coated. Transfer to 1-gallon resealable food storage bag.

2 Add powdered sugar to bag; seal bag and shake until well coated. Spread on waxed paper to cool. Store leftovers in airtight container in refrigerator.

Makes 4 servings

triple ginger cookies

2 cups all-purpose flour

2 teaspoons baking soda

1 teaspoon ground ginger

½ teaspoon salt

¾ cup (1½ sticks) dairy-free margarine

1¼ cups sugar, divided

¼ cup molasses

Prepared egg replacer equal to 1 egg

1 tablespoon grated fresh ginger

1 tablespoon finely minced crystallized ginger*

*Semisoft sugar-coated ginger slices are preferable to the small dry ginger cubes found on supermarket spice shelves. The softer, larger slices are available at natural foods or specialty stores. If using the small dry cubes of ginger, soak the cubes in boiling water a few minutes to soften, then drain, pat dry and mince.

1 Line cookie sheets with parchment paper. Sift flour, baking soda, ground ginger and salt into medium bowl.

2 Melt margarine in small saucepan over low heat; pour into large bowl and cool slightly. Add 1 cup sugar, molasses and egg replacer; mix well. Add flour mixture; mix well. Add fresh ginger and crystallized ginger; mix just until blended. Cover and refrigerate 1 hour.

3 Preheat oven to 375°F. Roll dough into 1-inch balls. Place remaining ¼ cup sugar in shallow dish; roll balls of dough in sugar to coat. Place 3 inches apart on prepared cookie sheets. (If dough is very sticky, drop by teaspoonfuls into sugar to coat.)

4 For chewy cookies, bake 7 minutes or until edges just start to brown. For crisper cookies, bake 9 to 11 minutes. Cool on cookie sheets 1 minute; remove to wire racks to cool completely.

Makes 3 dozen cookies

VARIATION: Roll dough in plastic wrap to form a log. Refrigerate up to one week or freeze up to two months. To bake, bring the dough nearly to room temperature and slice. Dip the tops in sugar and bake as directed.

almond-pear strudel

¾ cup slivered almonds

5 to 6 cups thinly sliced crisp pears (4 to 5 medium pears)

1 tablespoon grated lemon peel

1 tablespoon lemon juice

⅓ cup plus 1 teaspoon granulated sugar, divided

2 teaspoons ground cinnamon

1 teaspoon ground nutmeg

6 sheets (¼ pound) phyllo dough

¼ cup (½ stick) dairy-free margarine, melted

½ teaspoon almond extract

Powdered sugar (optional)

1 Preheat oven to 300°F. Spread almonds in shallow baking pan. Bake 6 to 8 minutes or until lightly browned, stirring frequently. Set aside.

2 Place sliced pears in large microwavable bowl. Stir in lemon peel and lemon juice. Microwave on HIGH 6 minutes or until tender; set aside to cool. Combine ⅓ cup granulated sugar, cinnamon and nutmeg in small bowl.

3 Cover work surface with plastic wrap. Place one phyllo sheet in center of plastic wrap. (Cover remaining phyllo dough with damp kitchen towel to prevent dough from drying out.) Brush phyllo sheet with 1 teaspoon margarine. Top with second sheet of phyllo dough; brush with 1 teaspoon margarine. Repeat layers with remaining phyllo dough.

4 *Increase oven temperature to 400°F.* Spray baking sheet with nonstick cooking spray. Drain pears; toss with sugar mixture and almond extract.

5 Spread pear mixture evenly over phyllo, leaving 3-inch strip on far long side. Sprinkle pears with ½ cup almonds. Brush strip with 2 teaspoons margarine. Beginning at long side of phyllo closest to you, carefully roll up jelly-roll style, using plastic wrap to gently lift dough. Place strudel, seam side down, on prepared baking sheet. Brush top with 1 teaspoon margarine.

6 Bake 20 minutes or until golden. Brush with remaining margarine; sprinkle with remaining ¼ cup almonds and 1 teaspoon granulated sugar. Bake 5 minutes. Cool 10 minutes before serving. Sprinkle with powdered sugar, if desired.

Makes 8 servings

cranberry coconut bars

2 cups fresh or frozen cranberries

1 cup dried sweetened cranberries

⅔ cup granulated sugar

¼ cup water

Grated peel of 1 lemon

1¼ cups all-purpose flour

¾ cup old-fashioned oats

½ teaspoon baking soda

½ teaspoon salt

1 cup packed brown sugar

¾ cup (1½ sticks) dairy-free margarine, softened

1 cup flaked coconut

1 cup chopped pecans, toasted*

*To toast pecans, spread in single layer on baking sheet. Bake in preheated 350°F oven 5 to 7 minutes or until golden brown, stirring frequently.

1 Preheat oven to 400°F. Grease and flour 13×9-inch baking pan.

2 Combine fresh cranberries, dried cranberries, granulated sugar, water and lemon peel in medium saucepan. Cook over medium-high heat 10 to 15 minutes or until cranberries begin to pop, stirring frequently. Mash cranberries with back of spoon. Let stand 10 minutes.

3 Combine flour, oats, baking soda and salt in medium bowl. Beat brown sugar and margarine in large bowl with electric mixer at medium speed until creamy. Add flour mixture; beat just until blended. Stir in coconut and pecans. Reserve 1½ cups; press remaining crumb mixture into bottom of prepared pan. Bake 10 minutes.

4 Gently spread cranberry filling evenly over crust. Sprinkle with reserved crumb mixture. Bake 18 to 20 minutes or until center is set and top is golden brown. Cool completely in pan on wire rack. Cut into bars.

Makes 2 dozen bars

NOTE: You can make these bars when fresh or frozen cranberries aren't available. Prepare the filling using 2 cups dried sweetened cranberries, 1 cup water and the grated peel of 1 lemon; cook 8 to 10 minutes over medium heat, stirring frequently. Use as directed in step 4.

tropic pops

2 bananas, cut into chunks

1½ cups unsweetened coconut milk

1½ cups pineapple juice

2 tablespoons sugar

½ teaspoon vanilla

⅛ teaspoon ground nutmeg

¼ cup sweetened flaked coconut

8 (5-ounce) plastic or paper cups or pop molds

8 pop sticks

1 Combine bananas, coconut milk, pineapple juice, sugar, vanilla and nutmeg in blender or food processor; blend until smooth. Stir in flaked coconut.

2 Pour mixture into cups. Cover top of each cup with small piece of foil. Freeze 2 hours.

3 Insert sticks through center of foil. Freeze 6 hours or until firm.

4 To serve, remove foil and gently twist pops out of plastic cups or peel away paper cups.

Makes 8 pops

TIP: For a ridged texture, use plastic cups.

all-american chocolate chip cookies

2 cups all-purpose flour

1 teaspoon baking soda

½ teaspoon salt

1 cup (2 sticks) dairy-free margarine

¾ cup packed brown sugar

½ cup granulated sugar

½ cup silken tofu, stirred until smooth

1 tablespoon vanilla

2 cups dairy-free semisweet chocolate chips

1 Preheat oven to 325°F. Line cookie sheets with parchment paper. Combine flour, baking soda and salt in medium bowl.

2 Beat margarine, brown sugar and granulated sugar in large bowl with electric mixer at medium speed until light and fluffy. Beat in tofu and vanilla. Add flour mixture; beat until combined. Stir in chocolate chips. Drop dough by heaping teaspoonfuls 2 inches apart onto prepared cookie sheets.

3 Bake 8 to 10 minutes or until light brown. Cool 2 minutes on cookie sheets; remove to wire racks to cool completely.

Makes about 4 dozen cookies

tropic pops

vegan birthday cake

3 cups all-purpose flour, plus additional for pans

2 cups sugar

6 tablespoons unsweetened cocoa powder

2 teaspoons baking soda

1 teaspoon salt

2 cups chocolate soymilk

½ cup plus 2 tablespoons vegetable oil

2 tablespoons cider vinegar

1 teaspoon vanilla

Chocolate No-Butter Buttercream Frosting (recipe follows)

1 Preheat oven to 350°F. Grease and flour two 9-inch round cake pans.

2 Whisk flour, sugar, cocoa, baking soda and salt in large bowl. Combine soymilk, oil, vinegar and vanilla in small bowl.

3 Add soymilk mixture to flour mixture; stir until smooth. Pour batter into prepared pans.

4 Bake 25 to 30 minutes or until toothpick inserted into centers comes out clean. (Center of cake may look darker than edges.) Cool in pans 5 minutes. Carefully invert onto wire racks to cool completely.

5 Meanwhile, prepare Chocolate No-Butter Buttercream Frosting. Fill and frost cake; decorate as desired.

Makes 10 servings

chocolate no-butter buttercream frosting

¾ cup (1½ sticks) dairy-free margarine

2 teaspoons vanilla

4 cups powdered sugar

½ cup unsweetened cocoa powder

4 to 6 tablespoons soy creamer

1 Beat margarine in large bowl with electric mixer at medium speed until light and fluffy. Beat in vanilla.

2 Gradually beat in powdered sugar and cocoa. Beat in soy creamer by tablespoonfuls until frosting reaches spreading consistency.

coconut milk ice cream

2 cans (about 14 ounces each) unsweetened coconut milk

½ cup sugar

1 dairy-free candy bar, crushed into small pieces

1 Combine coconut milk and sugar in medium saucepan. Cook over medium-low heat, whisking constantly, until sugar is dissolved and mixture is smooth. Refrigerate until cold.

2 Pour into ice cream maker; process according to manufacturer's directions, adding candy pieces during last 2 minutes. Transfer to freezer container and freeze until firm.

3 To serve, let ice cream soften at room temperature, or microwave on HIGH 20 to 30 seconds.

Makes about 1 quart

whole wheat brownies

½ cup whole wheat flour

½ teaspoon baking soda

¼ teaspoon salt

½ cup (1 stick) dairy-free margarine

1 cup packed brown sugar

½ cup unsweetened cocoa powder

½ cup silken tofu, stirred until smooth

½ cup dairy-free semisweet chocolate chips

1 teaspoon vanilla

1 Preheat oven to 350°F. Spray 8-inch square baking pan with nonstick cooking spray. Combine flour, baking soda and salt in small bowl.

2 Melt margarine in large saucepan over low heat. Add brown sugar; cook and stir about 4 minutes or until sugar is completely dissolved and mixture is smooth. Remove from heat. Sift in cocoa; stir until combined. Stir in flour mixture until smooth.

3 Sitr in tofu until smooth. Stir in chocolate chips and vanilla. Spoon batter into prepared pan.

4 Bake 25 minutes or until toothpick inserted into center comes out almost clean.

Makes 9 brownies

fudgy chocolate pudding cake

1 cup all-purpose flour

1 cup granulated sugar, divided

½ cup unsweetened cocoa powder, divided

2 teaspoons baking powder

¼ teaspoon salt

½ cup rice milk

6 tablespoons dairy-free margarine, melted

1 teaspoon vanilla

⅔ cup packed dark brown sugar

1¼ cups hot water

Vanilla dairy-free frozen dessert (optional)

1 Preheat oven to 350°F. Spray 8-inch square baking pan with nonstick cooking spray.

2 Combine flour, ¾ cup granulated sugar, ¼ cup cocoa, baking powder and salt in medium bowl. Beat in rice milk, margarine and vanilla until well blended. Spoon batter into prepared pan.

2 Combine remaining ¼ cup granulated sugar, ¼ cup cocoa and brown sugar in small bowl; mix well. Sprinkle mixture evenly over batter. Carefully pour hot water over batter. *Do not stir.*

3 Bake 25 to 35 minutes or until cake jiggles slightly when gently shaken. Remove from oven; let stand 15 minutes. Spoon into serving dishes; top with frozen dessert, if desired.

Makes 8 servings

cantaloupe sorbet

6 cups cubed fresh cantaloupe

⅓ cup light corn syrup

3 tablespoons lime juice

1 Place cantaloupe in food processor; process until puréed. Add corn syrup and lime juice; process until combined. Transfer to medium bowl; refrigerate until cold.

2 Pour into ice cream maker; process according to manufacturer's directions.

Makes 4 cups

fudgy chocolate pudding cake

METRIC CONVERSION CHART

VOLUME MEASUREMENTS (dry)

1/8 teaspoon = 0.5 mL
1/4 teaspoon = 1 mL
1/2 teaspoon = 2 mL
3/4 teaspoon = 4 mL
1 teaspoon = 5 mL
1 tablespoon = 15 mL
2 tablespoons = 30 mL
1/4 cup = 60 mL
1/3 cup = 75 mL
1/2 cup = 125 mL
2/3 cup = 150 mL
3/4 cup = 175 mL
1 cup = 250 mL
2 cups = 1 pint = 500 mL
3 cups = 750 mL
4 cups = 1 quart = 1 L

VOLUME MEASUREMENTS (fluid)

1 fluid ounce (2 tablespoons) = 30 mL
4 fluid ounces (1/2 cup) = 125 mL
8 fluid ounces (1 cup) = 250 mL
12 fluid ounces (1 1/2 cups) = 375 mL
16 fluid ounces (2 cups) = 500 mL

WEIGHTS (mass)

1/2 ounce = 15 g
1 ounce = 30 g
3 ounces = 90 g
4 ounces = 120 g
8 ounces = 225 g
10 ounces = 285 g
12 ounces = 360 g
16 ounces = 1 pound = 450 g

DIMENSIONS

1/16 inch = 2 mm
1/8 inch = 3 mm
1/4 inch = 6 mm
1/2 inch = 1.5 cm
3/4 inch = 2 cm
1 inch = 2.5 cm

OVEN TEMPERATURES

250°F = 120°C
275°F = 140°C
300°F = 150°C
325°F = 160°C
350°F = 180°C
375°F = 190°C
400°F = 200°C
425°F = 220°C
450°F = 230°C

BAKING PAN SIZES

Utensil	Size in Inches/Quarts	Metric Volume	Size in Centimeters
Baking or Cake Pan (square or rectangular)	8×8×2	2 L	20×20×5
	9×9×2	2.5 L	23×23×5
	12×8×2	3 L	30×20×5
	13×9×2	3.5 L	33×23×5
Loaf Pan	8×4×3	1.5 L	20×10×7
	9×5×3	2 L	23×13×7
Round Layer Cake Pan	8×1½	1.2 L	20×4
	9×1½	1.5 L	23×4
Pie Plate	8×1¼	750 mL	20×3
	9×1¼	1 L	23×3
Baking Dish or Casserole	1 quart	1 L	—
	1½ quart	1.5 L	—
	2 quart	2 L	—